Women OF POWER

THE INFLUENCE OF
Mother & Daughter

SUSAN EVANS MCCLOUD

T0398777

CFI
An imprint of Cedar Fort, Inc.
Springville, Utah

ISBN 13: 978-1-4621-4299-6

Published by CFI, an imprint of Cedar Fort, Inc.
2373 W. 700 S., Springville, UT 84663
Distributed by Cedar Fort, Inc., www.cedarfort.com

Library of Congress Control Number: 2022939022

Cover design by Courtney Proby
Cover design © 2022 Cedar Fort, Inc.

Printed in the United States of America

10 9 8 7 6 5 4 3 2 1

Printed on acid-free paper

This book is for

My sister, Jeannine George
Mother

Terri George Hodgen
Daughter

CONTENTS

INTRODUCTION

It may surprise us to realize that Susa Young Gates and her mother, Lucy Bigelow Young, lived in a time, and in an atmosphere, in which women were encouraged to develop their gifts and skills, to follow any noble and worthwhile pursuits that spoke to their hearts and awakened their spiritual desires.

Service was an essential ingredient of this pioneer era, and women's efforts flowed naturally in the many avenues of this direction. But always a woman was considered as a distinct and worthwhile individual. Those noble spirits who stood at the head of Relief Society, Young Women, and even Primary organizations took delight in their efforts to open doors of opportunity for every woman or girl within their sphere of influence.

Susa was especially gifted in this regard and spent much of her energy empowering and enlightening the young girls in the Church. Yes, they were definitely preparing for lives of usefulness. But lives of self-fulfillment were compatible with the quality of service the kingdom, and the Lord, desired at their hands! Respect for life, respect for womanhood, and faith in where our womanhood would lead us: these were the powerful eternal concepts taught to the receptive hearts of the women as they strived to learn and to lift themselves, day by day.

This standard—and the deep understanding and awareness that spring from it—is still a vital part of the workings of Heavenly Father's plan for His children. Do we understand it any better than they did? Surely we find ourselves struggling with the myriad distractions and worldly demands that compound our struggles and at times threaten to obscure the gentle, spiritual essence of our earthly existence.

This is why examples can be a delight, a blessing, and a hope to our hearts. Longfellow wrote, as quoted at the end of Susa's story, "Lives of great men all remind us we can make our lives sublime, and departing, leave behind us footprints on the sands of time."

The footprints of these two exceptional women are firm and deep, and to be trusted—especially since they were human, as obviously human and flawed as we find ourselves today. That is exactly what creates the magnificence and innate power of their contribution—and of ours—that out of weakness, error, fear, and even self-indulgence, *we can rise above. We can call upon the inner eternal Self of our Beings* and bring great and noble things to pass.

Mortal life is a most precious opportunity and a wonder in itself. Just thinking upon the words of Ralph Waldo Emerson helps us to realize this, for he said, "One moment in a man's life is a fact so stupendous as to take the luster from all fiction."[1]

You and I are works of wonder. I hope Lucy and Susa can lift us and help us celebrate what *we are,* what we have accomplished, and what increasingly gladsome, brave, and generous things we will yet accomplish with the tender, never-failing help of the Lord.

—Susan Evans McCloud

NOTE

1. https://lib.quotes.com//ralph-waldo-emerson-quotes/life

LUCY BIGELOW YOUNG

CHAPTER ONE

LIFE IS UNCERTAIN. THAT WAS ONE OF THE FIRST THINGS SHE HAD learned back in Nauvoo, and before.

Lucy walked down to the river, where the evening shadows were beginning to gather and the air had already grown still. She tried to picture David, but only living images would come to her mind, and these were more indistinct than she wished them to be. She could hear his voice playing over and over in her head. She felt herself tremble. There had been other men interested in her—both young and old. Her parents always maintained that she was the prettiest girl in the family, which was intended to mean something, she supposed.

She had always felt pretty when David looked at her in that intense, gentle way. He loved her; he had told her he loved her, even in Nauvoo, before they journeyed to Winter Quarters. They were to be married as soon as he returned from Wisconsin, where his mother owned some property and he was being sent to ascertain conditions there. His going seemed a bit vague to Lucy, as did her promise to marry him upon his return. She was young still, and she felt young. And after the terrors her family had suffered in Nauvoo, Winter Quarters did not seem much better. There were still so few homes, only tents that the winds tried to blow down. There was so much mud, so much sickness, and so little food. And yet, she tried to remind herself, at least here there was peace.

David was given a blessing before he left, and that had been a comfort. But why did he tease and halfway distress her by saying, "When I get back, Lucy, I'll probably find you married to some old man."[1]

He knew what she had asserted over and over again: she would never give herself to a man who was older and already married—to one woman or more.

Lucy bent down and picked a small bunch of half-wilted mint, loosening it from the moist soil, pressing the greening leaves between her fingers, and drawing in the strong, clean smell. Against her will she remembered another thing from David's blessing. He had been told he would serve a mission preaching to spirits in prison. No one thought much of the words when they were spoken, with their minds on other, more immediate things. But the world of spirits—that could mean but one thing. And was that truly where he was supposed to go?

Oh, David! Why? Why did you have to go now? Did you know you would never come back to the Saints, back to me? Lucy cried the words within her own heart, but she made no sound. *Measles!* What a useless waste of a young life whose promise was like the fresh wind that swept over the muddy streets and fields of the quarters, Winter Quarters, crowded with weary, struggling, disposed Saints.

She sighed. It was time to go back to help prepare a frugal meal and do chores that were waiting. Lucy did not mind work, and right now work would be for her a salvation of sorts. She liked being helpful. She liked having something of real purpose to occupy her hands. Suddenly, against her will, her mind began stubbornly drawing pictures out from the dark, jumbled memories of their last days in Illinois. It was difficult for her to forget the fear that had tightened her body with every breath and the expression of horrified disbelief that seemed permanently stamped on her father's features.

But her father had not died. And, save for the little children whom the Lord had taken from them, all the family were safely here with the Saints. No matter what the challenges and conditions, this was a good place to be. She was grateful; she would be as grateful as she could be. That would help.

Lucy was born at Charleston, which sat in the backwoods of Coles County, Illinois, on October 3, 1830, only a few short months after Joseph Smith had organized The Church of Jesus Christ in Fayette. Her mother was Mary Gibbs, born on June 26, 1809, in Lisle, Broome County, New York, and her father Nahum Bigelow, who had been born on February 19, 1785, to parents who were farmers in Brandon, Vermont. She was the second daughter to enter the family, after Mary, who had been named for their mother. Their home was a modest cabin consisting of two rooms.

The history of her parents is nearly as captivating as fiction, and both proved themselves to be distinct individuals who knew their own minds.

Nahum, with what Susa called "Yankee restlessness,"[2] decided to see something of the world before settling down. He traveled light, with little more than a backpack, enjoying the experiences and people he met. At length he found himself in Lawrenceville, Illinois, where he unexpectedly met a girl, a very young girl only twelve years of age, who, without warning, entirely entranced him. Her face was intelligent, yet the lines were sensitive, too, and her eyes were the darkest, deepest blue he had ever seen. He said, "If ever I marry, that's the girl I want for my wife."[3]

Mary was twelve, and Nahum was thirty-six years old, certainly old enough to have been her father! A variety of things must have attracted her to him and convinced her that she was safe, and would be happy placing her life in his hands.

She certainly was not afraid of either work or responsibility, a trait which her daughter, Lucy, most definitely inherited. When she was ten, Mary's mother spent months going about, boarding from place to place, doing weaving for the households where she temporarily stayed. Mary was left to see to things in her absence: cooking, candle dipping, washing, and even planting and caring for a garden and preserving the produce as the summer months waned. What is more, her baby brother was only a year and a half!

She was able, however, to ease into her relationship with Nahum, through a period of boarding school, as well as during the trauma of her fifteenth summer when she was extremely ill with whooping cough and scarlet fever. Nahum came over, usually once a month, to visit her, until she was nearly sixteen when he finally proposed marriage. He had surely meant what he had said, that this was the one he wanted to have for his wife. They were married on December 2, 1826.

By the time Lucy was born, they had moved to Coles County. Shortly after their fifth child, Lovina, was born in March 1834, they were visited by missionaries from The Church of Jesus Christ of Latter-day Saints. Much Bible reading and thoughtful prayer ensued, though Mary was the first to accept this new doctrine and hold it patiently in her heart. It took four years before they moved, in 1843, gathering with the Saints just eighteen miles outside Nauvoo.

Their years of persecution would be a story in themselves. But they culminated in an unusual way. To escape the keen eye of the mobsters who were constantly watching and harassing them, Nahum left the farm for a season in the care of his son, Asa. As the harvest approached, he returned to help the boy gather in their crops.

His friends warned Nahum, but he took no heed and was pleasantly surprised by the apparent kindness he encountered when he went back. A non-Mormon neighbor by the name of Sam Porter invited him to breakfast, and Nahum foolishly accepted. He noticed the unusual bitterness of the coffee but thought little of it, until his return to his own house when he was suddenly overcome with an excruciating pain.

Asa, terrified, drove his father into Nauvoo. His granddaughter Susa later described the horrifying scene:

> His distress was beyond description. His screams were heard at a great distance, and scarcely could the people about him hold him in his terrible struggles for life and breath. Medical skill acknowledged itself powerless. Again and again was he administered to by the Elders of the Church, and at length the evil was in part rebuked, and he began to be more able to endure his suffering. All winter, however, he was very ill and "knew that it was God, and the power of God only, which gave him back his life for a little season."[4]

They went on, as did so many others, one step, one hope, and one prayer at a time. A son was born to Nahum and Mary on the Fourth of July, only a week after the Prophet and Hyrum were killed in Carthage. They named the child Joseph Smith Bigelow, but his

sweet, promising life lasted scarcely over nine months, and the grieving family had to prepare for his body a small, lonely grave, which
soon they would be leaving behind.

All this and more was in Lucy's memory and heart as she left the
quiet bank of the Missouri and walked back to where her loved ones
waited, struggling with her own questions and sorrows, but somehow
comforted and strengthened, though she was not certain quite how.

Though Winter Quarters served the Saints as headquarters for the
Church, this role was to last for a little less than a year. But organization was always a gift with the Latter-day Saints, and by the end of
1846 a large stockade had been built, as well as seven hundred houses
of various quality and design, from dugouts hugging the bluffs, to
homes with roofs and floors, some of these even boasting two stories
and wooden floors. Yet, much of the suffering endured by all came
from the wretched conditions the Saints endured while crossing the
state of Iowa. They faced terrible winds and merciless exposure to the
elements, along with lack of sufficient food and needed nutrition—
only to meet the devastation of malaria on their weakened systems
once they arrived in camp. Consequently, several hundred Saints,
many of these babies and young children, perished during that winter
of 1846–47.

At this time the Bigelow family had a snug cabin into which
Brigham Young was welcomed by Nahum, who was anxious for the
President's counsel concerning his daughters. Apparently a Brother
Wicks had approached him, wanting both of his girls for wives. Lucy,
being somewhat impetuous and outspoken, re-confirmed her oft-stat-
ed stand that she would never marry a married man. And Mary hung
back from accepting such a proposal, as well, despite his unrelenting
persistence.

Brother Wicks happened to be working for the President at this
time, and Brigham's response was interesting. "Well, so far as anything I know, brother Wicks is a very good man, but his wife is a

high-strung piece. Let the matter rest awhile, and I will come up and see the girls about it before long."[5]

The busy prophet went out of his way to spend evenings in the Bigelow home, getting to know the girls. Mary was complacently there, but Lucy was generally absent. Though both girls were somewhat reticent and shy in the great man's presence, at last Mary warned Lucy that he wanted her to make up her mind. "So what do you say?" she pressed.

"I don't know. I'll tell you what it is, Mary. I don't feel as if I could marry him. He's got such lots of wives now, and it don't seem like he could ever be my husband."

Yet, according to Lucy's daughter Susa, when Brigham appeared the next Sunday and asked outright whether she wished to be sealed to him, the following occurred: "'Y-es sir,' faltered the little coward, and her fate was sealed forever, thank God!"[6]

In the evening of March 14, 1846, President Young, along with Elders Kimball, Willard Richards, and Ezra T. Benson arrived at the Bigelow cabin. Mary and Lucy stood solemnly to be sealed to this tall, genial man, while Elder Kimball officiated in the sacred covenant, perhaps seemingly out of place in the low-roofed cabin, lit only by the warm flames of tallow candles and a low fire place. First Brigham took Mary's hand, then Lucy's, as the sisters were sealed to him, "clad in dark homespun, and decked only in the sweet, faint blushes of innocence."[7]

Reality quickly set in. Brigham was preparing to lead the first hand-picked company of Saints to the Rocky Mountains. Lucy was restless. She was always happiest when she was busiest. Without having details, we do know that she, her mother, and a brother traveled to St. Louis, where they were able to find employment and where Lucy learned to do hand-turned work on fine ladies' gowns.

When Brigham returned from the Salt Lake Valley and learned that his young wife had gone off to St. Louis, he responded that "he would rather have given the last coat off his back than to have her down there."[8]

The three dutifully returned, bringing a large amount of much-needed supplies and a determination to make this trip only as a visit to Winter Quarters, for they wished and intended to return. But when

President Young asked Lucy if she would not rather return to the Valley with him, she replied rather meekly, "If you wish me to."

"I would much rather you would," was his forceful reply. But then he added, "I am very thankful to say that I have heard a very good report of you while you stayed in St. Louis, but I don't wish you to go down there again."[9]

Brigham, required to use his own teams and wagons for Church business, arranged for Lucy to travel with this same company that was soon to leave, starting out in May of 1848. He had found place for her in the wagon of Brother McMullen, where she would be able to assist his wife, who was an invalid, and in doing so help to pay her way. President Young also contributed a quantity of flour and a yoke of oxen to add to the bargain.

Lucy parted from her loved ones and, alone with strangers, was now, she realized, to be the first of her family to make the journey through desert and hazardous mountain reaches to an unknown valley somewhere in the distance, which was to become her home.

NOTES

1. Susa Young Gates, "Sketch of Nahum Bigelow," *Juvenile Instructor*, 15 April 1891. Edited by Dan Forward, 1997, 1.
2. Ibid., 1.
3. Ibid., 5.
4. Ibid.
5. Susa Young Gates, "From Impulsive Girl to Patient Wife, Lucy Bigelow Young," *Utah Historical Quarterly*, vol. 45, number 3, 1977. By *Utah State History*, 1.
6. Ibid., 2.
7. Ibid., 2.
8. Ibid., notes, 2.
9. Ibid., 3.

Chapter Two

———— ✦ ————

Perhaps this was the first pivotal point in young Lucy's life, when critical choices and decisions would begin to determine her way. She had agreed to become the wife of a married man, something she had been sure she would never agree to do. But perhaps the rather extreme diversity of years between her father and her mother carried an influence, for Mary was thirteen, she states, when she met Nahum Bigelow, and he was thirty-seven—making him twenty-four years older than she! Yet Lucy had seen the happiness and devotion of the life they shared.

Lucy wanted action, but she also wanted security. She wasn't afraid, but she was uncertain. The life before *her* would contain differences and challenges she had no way of anticipating. With the uncanny wisdom of her nature she decided that if she was going to be happy in this large, diverse, family, the only way to do so would be to make herself *useful.* And this meant opening her heart and looking for something good in every person she met and in every place in which she found herself. This resolve, as she expressed it at one time to her daughter, Susa, was that "early in her marriage, for her own peace of mind, she would not lower herself to backbite or criticize anyone, particularly her husband, if children were around. Susa remembered that her mother rarely said anything negative about anyone in the family."[1]

She began at the beginning. Soon after the pioneer company started off, she discovered a pleasing companion in Ellen Rockwood, another young wife of her husband's. It was natural for the two girls to slip away from the noises of animals and the confusion of children to walk alone by themselves, either to linger behind the others or to forge out ahead.

To her chagrin, Lucy became suddenly so ill that President Young came quickly to their wagon to administer to her. The next morning her skin was sprinkled all over with measles, and she knew from whence the weakness and fever had come.

Her first defined challenge also came suddenly upon her when Sister McMullen said, "Lucy, you are going to be asked to work for Vilate Decker this winter for your board."

With a flare of her characteristic stubbornness, Lucy replied, "Well, I won't do it, let me tell you."[2] She had heard, as everyone had, how proud and haughty, how disagreeable this woman was.

Brigham, learning of Lucy's response, knew at once what she needed. He came to the wagon and asked for a moment with her alone. Then he "talked long and kindly to her, telling his girl-bride about the delicate health of his daughter Vilate and of his fears that she would die prematurely as her mother had done."[3]

Lucy's heart was as warm as it was impulsive. How could she have resisted? Perhaps she remembered the stories of how tenderly the young Brigham had cared for his invalid wife, rising early each morning to get breakfast for her and the two little girls, dressing himself and the children, cleaning and tidying up where necessary, and then gently settling Miriam in her rocking chair beside the fireplace and walking out to face his own work of the day.

Upon his return he would "cook a meal for the family, finish up the household labors, see to the needs of his daughters, and put both wife and children to bed. For all Brigham knew, this would be the pattern of his days for long years to come. He accepted the limitations and disappointments nobly, concentrating on the opportunities placed in his path, loving and serving as his mother, in her own patience and gentleness, had taught him to do."[4] He had watched his mother die of the same dread consumption when he was only a boy of fourteen, and now the nightmare was replaying itself in his life. He could not even have dreamed of the overwhelming power of leadership, of the intense weight of responsibility that was to be his. And this trial was perhaps the first proving of the Lord's servant, Brigham, in the eyes of his Heavenly Father, who was carefully watchful of the unfolding of his life.

This insight into the spirit of the man she had married was important to Lucy, as well. She promised to do as he asked, and as the times of their association passed she grew to love his daughter as if she were her own sister.

Most of the Saints living in Winter Quarters left for the Salt Lake Valley that May, the first company consisting of 2,500 people. Brigham remained for seventeen days longer to oversee the departure of the last company and then left with his counselors and their families in a group that consisted of just over eight hundred wagons, as well as all the needed stock and supplies. Before the year had found its way to an end, three thousand additional Saints had swelled the number to over five thousand now gathered together in the pristine valley the Lord had prepared for them.

What shelter did they find during those first weeks and months? Lucy was given place in a little house made of adobe, actually the first in the Valley, and built by President Young himself. Here she lived with Vilate Decker, her husband and little girl, and two of Brigham's other young wives squeezed in, Margaret Alley and Emmeline Free. As soon as possible their husband built the Log Row, with the doors of the seven or eight bedrooms opening on the south side. Even here Lucy shared one of these rooms with Clara Decker, "who became one of her truest and best loved friends."[5]

They were well situated compared to many in the Valley, and shelter was not the only problem the people faced. As President George A. Smith candidly recorded, "For the next three years we were reduced to considerable straits for food. Fast meetings were held, and contributions constantly made for those who had no provisions. Every head of a family issued rations to those dependent upon him . . . rawhides, wolves, rabbits, thistle roots, sage roots, and everything that could be thought of that would preserve lift were resorted to . . . a great deal of the grain planted here the first year grew only a few inches high; it was so short it could not be cut, the people had to pull it."[6] Brigham put his own family on a ration of half a pound each daily—but he assured them, and all the Saints, that this place was exactly where the

Lord had put them and wanted them, and it would "become one of the most productive places in the world."[7]

Brigham's motto for the household, often articulated for them and for his people, became instilled time after time into the minds and wills of the women and children who were in Brigham's special care. "Instead of crying over our sufferings, as some seem inclined to do, I would rather tell a good story and leave the crying to others," he always maintained. "I do not know that I have ever suffered. I do not realize it."[8] Again he stated: "The Lord has led this people through scenes of sorrow and affliction. . . . I can say that I do not consider that I have ever suffered anything for this kingdom—nothing in the least."[9] And, pinpointing the very heart of his sacred convictions, Brigham told his people, "As to trials, well bless your hearts, the man or woman who enjoys the spirit of our religion has no trials!"[10]

The spirit of their religion, of the restored gospel of Jesus Christ, embedded itself deeply into the spirit of the young woman who had determined to make her life one of usefulness, of service, and—perhaps not even fully realized by herself—of joy.

Lucy's parents did not arrive in the Valley until 1849. Mary, who had also been sealed to President Young, never actually became his wife. Lucy wrote letters to her during this time, trying to draw pictures of her life and the lives of the other wives in Brigham's family. But Mary continued to demur and eventually divorced him, never actually living with him and eventually marrying two other men.

Lucy did not become a proper or "bona fide wife" until 1850, so she was now twenty years old and much matured by the experiences of the last few years. She had also observed this man who was her husband in a wide variety of circumstances and challenges. As Susa explained things years later, "When the Spirit of the Lord whispered to (Brigham Young) that he should seek such and such a one for a wife, he did so in a quiet, manly, grave way, never with any spirit of co-ercion on his part, and always leaving as he so often expressed it, 'the sparking to come after. Marry first and spark after,' was a favorite aphorism of his, and he carried it out in his own life."[11]

Lucy saw and felt this, and gained a quiet assurance of it. Susa always maintained that she never heard her father speak a harsh or unkind word to any of his wives. Susa's observation of this fact is almost lyrical:

> His beautiful courtesy was never more in evidence than when he approached any one of his wives whom he loved and who loved him. Especially was that so when in the company of Mother Young, whose health was rather poor and who had born the heat and burden of the day for him and with him. To her he paid exquisite attention, quiet, composed but sincere. His attitude of consideration towards her was reflected in that of every other wife and child he had. . . . He was so eminently successful in his home life that no one ever related to him, or who benefited from his friendship, ever failed to return in full the measure he gave of love, heaped and running over.[12]

Ellis Shipp, who went on to become the second woman doctor in Utah, delivering over six thousand babies and lifting the already high standard of medicine in the state, lived in the Beehive House with some of Brigham's family for an extended period. She observed that "here there were no discords. This home circle was the pattern of comfort, order and refinement—the abode of love, sweet peace, and divine progression, the blessed offspring of a supreme faith, noble industry, and beautiful unselfishness."[13]

Expanding this already lavish praise, Ellis added: "How kind and fatherly Brigham Young was to me. My heart warms and my eyes moisten to the big heart, the generous consideration of that great man, who lived to bless all the world as far as mortal power could reach. Directed by what seemed a divine instinct he could read and understand the human heart. His vision could encompass all of mortal need in the great and vital things, and even unto the smallest detail of everyday life."[14]

In this rare atmosphere Lucy's own gifts flourished, and her understanding and inner contentment grew.

Brigham Young's households were carefully structured and organized. Each woman had her own responsibilities and tasks. Several of the wives were involved in candle dipping, since twenty bedrooms for which to provide light was a prodigious amount. And during these earlier years Lucy milked the eleven cows belonging to the household. She had been raised on a farm and was fond of the beasts, discovering as only a little girl how to carefully and patiently get the cows to "give down" their milk for her.

Susa explains that this was during the period when grasshoppers were still plaguing the Saints. Throughout the Valley wives worked at the grim task alongside their husbands, and Lucy was willingly one of them.

All these many years later, we tend to think in sweet, loving terms of the seagulls coming to save the pioneers. We have no real concept of what they went through. But the devastation of crickets was powerfully described by John R. Young:

> Oh how we fought and prayed and battled against the myriads of black, loathsome insects that flowed down like a flood of filthy water from the mountainside . . . the crickets would climb the stalk, bite off the head, then come down and eat it. . . . The first I knew of the gulls, I heard their sharp cry. . . . I have been asked how numerous were the gulls? There must have been thousands of them. Their coming was like a great cloud; and when they passed between us and the sun, a shadow covered the field.
>
> "I could see the gulls settling for more than a mile around us. As I remember it, the gulls came every morning for about three weeks, when their mission was apparently ended, and they ceased coming. The precious crops were saved.[15]

The Beehive House was the first of Brigham's homes completed, followed by the White House, positioned a bit up the hill. "Mother Young," as everyone affectionately called Mary Ann Angell, was moved into the comfort of that home, and Lucy Decker Young was established as feminine head of the Beehive House, where she was challenged with feeding the twenty-odd workers as well as her own family, and often helping to entertain Brigham's distinguished guests, as well.

The Lion House came together more slowly. It was designed and constructed to be a home for ten so-called "girl wives," though some already had given birth to a child or two. Lucy was among that number. Her first daughter, Eudora, was born in the Log Row on May 12, 1852. The conditions were rather primitive, with ropes stretched on pegs to support a cotton tick filled with straw. But the joy and wonder were not affected by minor circumstances such as these.

The Lion House was not yet completed when it came time for Lucy's second child to be born. At her husband's invitation, she selected one of the sitting rooms to be her own. Then he ordered, in the early days of March, that the floor be hurriedly laid. While this was being seen to, Lucy herself was fretting about the condition of the men who were working long, punishing hours in order to see the task done. In Susa's words: "Mother's heart bled for the hungry workmen who were crowding the completion of the Lion House, and many days she carried over her share of the scanty rations of bread and skim milk to the weakened carpenters and painters who labored all winter to finish this unique dwelling place."[16]

All was ready just in time, and on March 18, 1856, Susa was born. That is Susa or Susannah, or Susan. Her name became a point of humorous disagreement between husband and wife for years. Brigham had a sister Susannah, named after the sister of his mother, Abigail. Had he really chosen that for the baby's name? Nothing definitive was ever decided between them.

Sister Zina acted as family midwife at the birth. When she told Lucy that she had a little girl, the mother's unexpected reaction was, "Shucks!"

Zina responded with gentle emphasis: "No, it isn't all shucks, it's wheat and full weight too."[17]

Throughout her life, Susa tended to joke about the story, deriding herself as "shucks" when she did something foolish, or not admirable, or not what she wanted it to be. But it seems this was also a kind of standard that kept her to the highest within herself.

There was much going on among the Saints from March of 1856 to the spring of 1858. On July 24, 1847, a large number of the Saints were gathered to celebrate the day. The pilgrimage began on July 22 with 2,487 people, nearly five hundred carriages and wagons, as well as a thousand horses and nearly four hundred oxen and cows all lumbering up to the Silver Lake resort in Cottonwood Canyon. Plank floors had been laid for dancing, and five bands and several choirs were getting ready to perform. Hundreds and hundreds of people were laughing, greeting one another, celebrating the miracle of ten years away from the persecution and cruelty which they had known, feeling hopeful and grateful.

"But with dramatic cruelty, more cruel in life than in the greatest fiction, at high noon four solemn messengers—travel-worn horsemen who had ridden long and hard—entered the camp: A.O. Smoot, Porter Rockwell, Judson Stoddard, and Elias Smith. They brought news that an army of twenty-five hundred were marching toward the territory, by order of President Buchanan himself."[18]

Wild accusations, largely from Judge Drummond, whose infamous, immoral behavior had become almost legendary, incited even further action. The President of the United States appointed a new governor without even informing the old, cancelled the mail contract, and listened to strident voices from men who had only their own interests at heart.

It is difficult to imagine the stunned atmosphere and the immediate fears and anxieties that arose in the hearts of that great throng. Immediate action would be necessary, and the Saints, gathering in the tabernacle on August 19, pledged their support to whatever course was decided. Brigham, well aware of the irony, on August 20 recorded: "The Day I entered Salt Lake Valley 24 July 1847 I remarked—if the devil will let me alone for 10 years—we will bid them defiance. July 24 1857—10 years to a day—first heard of the intender expedition to Utah under Genl. Harney. I feel the same now. I defy all the powers of darkness."[19]

The Utah War, or the Echo Canyon War, as it is called, is most certainly a story in itself. There is no doubt of the great amount of praying done in Brigham Young's households as the prophet managed, through skillful maneuvering and the grace of God, to harass and curtail the army, without pitched battles or bloodshed. His strategy shone with a powerful purpose and sincerity, as evidenced when he told the army and the government after much negotiation, friendly and otherwise, and with the aid of the Saints' true friend, Colonel Kane, that the soldiery could march through Salt Lake City without any pauses or stops and establish a camp, being at least forty miles away. The homes were ready—furniture piled and kindling in place— with a man or young boy in every one, and they would be put to the torch if a single soldier stepped out of line. Four thousand hands had been raised in the tabernacle to support this decision.

The Saints had suffered as bitterly as flesh and spirit can in Missouri, Kirtland, and then Missouri again, culminating with their expulsion from the beloved city of Nauvoo, leaving their slain Prophet and Patriarch, and the just-completed temple behind. Yes, they would rather go up into the fastness of the mountains and hide with the natives there than to see the fruits of their love and toil either destroyed or inhabited by enemies once again.

It was not easy to follow the prophet's counsel and move bed and board over the high point of the mountain to the small settlement of Provo. Wilford Woodruff left as late as April 7 but encountered a severe snowstorm, which caused much inconvenience and suffering. But Lucy, knowing the importance of action and wanting to be in the forefront, doing rather than waiting, put her little household in order at once so that she was actually the first of the wives ready to go. Brigham had asked Zina, who was a born leader, to take the lead in organizing and moving his family along, and when he learned of Lucy's readiness he was happy to have her accompany this sister wife whom she loved and admired so well.

We have almost no details of what the journey and its day-to-day particulars were like. We do know, thanks to Susa's account, that there was no room to be found for their family in the small Provo village. Every home and building was crowded to the gills with refugees; even the cattle and other animals were packed into yards and open corals while the people commandeered the protection of the barns.

The only suggestion, almost ludicrous in its absurdity, was a little hut that housed a tame bear. "'Let's try it.' And try it they did! With the Bishop to lead, the two boys to drive the bear out and to clean out the stable refuse, and the two mother wives to clean and purify—with cakes of home-made soap and plenty of lye made by the wood ashes— they soon scrubbed out and cleaned everything that was scrubbable, and by nightfall, a few boards were made into a hasty bed frame, supporting the straw ticks and feather beds."[20]

The noble, enterprising women did not have to make do for long. Once Brigham made his appearance, he immediately began to build a simple house large and roomy enough to accommodate his family. The Lion House was closed up; all of Salt Lake City was closed up as the Saints waited on the Lord. Two of Lucy's brothers, Asa and Hiram, had been living in Davis County but came down during the move and remained in Provo. Lucy's mother, Mary Gibbs Bigelow, was by this time a widow, but she had many married children to watch over her and help her now that she was alone.

As soon as things were settled with the government officials, Brigham prepared to return home, giving the people the option to follow him if they liked. Lucy returned in the fall and, though exhausted, continued her usual routine—doing her share of the work and helping anyone who needed her. After the winter, the cumulative effects took their toll on her—these and the strain and disappointment of what Susa called "many pre-mature birth mishaps."[21]

To be virtually bedridden, to be unable to keep her hands and heart busy was a great trial for Lucy. As she recovered bit by bit she cherished more than ever her woman's strength, and the many times that strength, and her willing heart, had been a blessing to those in need of her help.

NOTES

1. *Brigham Young Homes*, edited Colleen Whitley (Logan, Utah: Utah State University Press, 2002), 82.
2. Susa Young Gates "From Impulsive Girl to Patient Wife: Lucy Bigelow Young," *Utah Historical Quarterly*, Vol. 45, Number 3, 1977.
3. Ibid.
4. Ibid.
5. Ibid.
6. Susa Young Gates and Leah D. Widtsoe, *The Life Story of Brigham Young* (New York: The Macmillan Company, 1931), 123–24.
7. Ibid., 123–24.
8. *Journal of Discourses*, volume 8, 67.
9. Ibid., 67.
10. Widtsoe, *Discourses of Brigham Young*, 348.

11. Gates, "From Impulsive Girl to Patient Wife: Lucy Bigelow Young," 23.

12. Gates and Widtsoe, *The Life Story of Brigham Young*, 340.

13. Susan Evans McCloud, *Brigham Young, a Personal Portrait* (American Fork, Utah: Covenant Communications, 1996), 242.

14. McCloud, *Not In Vain: The Inspiring story of Ellis Shipp: Pioneer Woman Doctor* (Salt Lake City: Bookcraft, 1984), 52.

15. Gates and Widtsoe, *The Life Story of Brigham Young*, 118.

16. Robyn A. "The 13th Apostle-Susa Young Gates: The Gift of Giving Life," the-thirteenth-apostle-susa-young-gates.

17. Ibid.

18. Susan Evans McCloud, Brigham Young: A *Personal Portrait* (American Fork, Utah: Covenant Communications, 1996), 199–200.

19. Secretary's Journal, 2 August, 1857, *Brigham Young Papers*, LDS Church Archives, 201.

20. Gates, "From Impulsive Girl to Patient Wife: Lucy Bigelow Young," 5.

21. Ibid.

CHAPTER THREE

———— ❧ ————

It was now spring of 1859. Lucy was in her twenty-ninth year, with just two little daughters of her own. The busyness of her life and its many demands kept her mind off herself. The family's routine included Sabbath meetings twice a day in the tabernacle, as well as an evening ward meeting, Thursday fast meetings, and morning prayer, private to each wife in the sanctity of her own sitting room. These were meaningful to Lucy, and she did not mind observing them meticulously.

But there were other things besides work. She was often called upon to organize parties or picnics in the warm months. And, once her skill as a seamstress was discovered, Lucy was invited to design and create costumes for the theatre. She loved to sew, and she had an eye for the subtle little touches and decorations that would make a dress stand out and be remembered. "She could," as Susa liked to boast, "make a dress fit the wearer's waist like a glove. She was wont to refer, with some pride, to her tailor's training in St. Louis before coming to the Valley."[1]

Lucy became the assistant to Sister Bowring, who recognized her artistic skills and her determination to not cease until everything she did was as a perfectly done as possible. This extended to a rather informal, unexpected role as official hairdresser for Brigham's older daughters who were often called "The Big Ten." They enjoyed many privileges, including a carriage for their own use and an enchanting sleigh for winter passage along the snowy roads. He gave them thoughtful gifts, including pretty sashes, which were the fashion, to wear to the theatre.

He was aware of their needs and kept an open-door policy with his children: they knew that if they really needed him they could enter his office unannounced and he would interrupt himself and see to their needs. The harmony inherent in this made their mothers' hearts glad.

Theatre was considered a good, wholesome entertainment for the community. Brigham supported it and even allowed his daughters to take acting parts. Many famous actresses and actors performed in Salt Lake, including Julia Dean Hayne, Phil Margetts, the much-loved Maude Adams, and as time went on, Maurice Barrymore, father of John and Lionel.

Years after the theatre had been in operation in the city, Brigham Young said, "If I were placed on a cannibal island and given a task of civilizing its people, I should straightway build a theatre for the purpose."[2]

It was Lucy's habit to attend at least one performance of each play that was produced on the stage, being there for first nights, if possible, and sometimes two or three times during the week. She must have felt a quiet satisfaction in her own contributions that added to the beauty and overall harmony of the play.

Dancing was another form of entertainment much encouraged by the prophet, who said: "The world considers it very wicked for a Christian to hear music and to dance. Many preachers say that fiddling and music come from hell; but I say there is no fiddling, there is no music in hell. Music belongs to heaven, to cheer God, angels and men. If we could hear the music there is in heaven, it would overwhelm us mortals."[3]

He further expounded: "I want it distinctly understood, that fiddling and dancing are no part of our worship. What are they for then? . . . That my body may keep pace with my mind . . . this is the reason why I am so fond of these pastimes—they give me a privilege to throw everything off, and shake myself, that my body may exercise, and my mind rest."[4]

Lucy loved to dance. Susa describes her as "a graceful, stately figure on the floor, with her dainty ruffled skirts billowing about her as she danced."[5] She danced with some of the older boys, or friends who were present, as well as with her husband.

Captain Stansbury had been sent to the Valley by the Army Corp of Topographical Engineers, and perhaps his greatest accomplishment in his time here was a four-week circumnavigation of the Great Salt Lake. One on occasion, after attending a ball in Salt Lake in the spring of 1854, he left a delightful description of what he experienced and saw: "A larger collection of fairer and more beautiful women I never saw in one room. All of them were dressed in white muslin, some with pink and others with blue sashes. Flowers were the only ornament in the hair. The utmost order and the strictest decorum prevailed. Polkas and waltzes were not danced; country dances, cotillions, quadrilles, etc., were permitted."[6]

Camp Floyd did not remain for long, yet even the three years it existed had a demoralizing effect among the young people, some of whom were drawn to the "forbidden fruits," the excitement and even danger of a world so outside their own.

But in this, as in all things, Heavenly Father's purposes were brought to pass. The Fort was in the wastes of Cedar Valley, thirty-six miles from Salt Lake City. Interestingly, Brigham had offered Colonel Johnston a spot in the lush, much more habitable Cache Valley, but in bile and resentment, Johnston declined. He could not, however, help describing it as "this infernal region—it is to me worse than any imagined horrors of a Siberian exile."[7]

A search of histories revealed the amazing fact that "59 Civil War generals—30 for the Union and 29 for the Confederacy—earlier served as junior officers in the 'Utah War' or at the camp Floyd it created. . . Generals who rose from Camp Floyd's ranks fought in virtually every major battle of the war, from Fort Sumter to Appomattox, including 20 who faced each other at Gettysburg alone!"[8]

But, as far as the Saints were concerned, the end of their three-year ordeal brought unexpected blessings. When the Civil War broke out, the army was recalled and the camp abandoned. Their amassment of goods had to be abandoned and sacrificed. For example, "hundreds of wagons valued at $150 to $175 were sold for $10 each. Flour, purchased by the government for $28.40 a sack, sold for fifty-two cents."[9]

Many of the officers called upon President Young before they departed, and some even left written descriptions praising the characteristics and behavior of the Mormon prophet. But Brigham and Colonel Johnston never met face to face. Johnston was killed in the Battle of Shiloh, fighting against the forces of General Grant.

Perhaps it was Lucy's milking skills that recommended her, for in 1862 she went down to the family farm in order to make cheese and butter for the Lion House family, and to care for the men who worked there.

There was a separate milk and cheese house at the farm connected by a roofed passage to what was the cook house and dining room. Lucy's bedroom was above the area where she worked. The house was built near a spring, and down in the cellar was a well that tapped into the spring. This was in a separate part from the storage area where many foods, as well as the dairy products, were kept.

After the cream in the milk rose, it was skimmed off and churned. "Usually the night milk had the cream and was used for churning, and the morning milk was used fresh, still slightly warm for breakfast. Churning the butter took about twenty minutes. . . . Once the butter formed, the buttermilk was drained off and the butter was rinsed in clear water."[10] Salt was worked into the butter that was churned with a large wooden paddle before being stored in the cool cellar, much of it transported into the city for the waiting family there.

It was a joy to be invited to eat a meal there, where fresh vegetables, fresh fruit in cream, and roast turkey were often served. "The Forest Farm was considered the best farmhouse on the best farm in the valley."[11]

The farm had room enough for all the children to gather for holidays and all sorts of festivities. Susa remembered, "Sometimes father would have a party for us all when we stayed the night, making beds on the floor, girls sleeping with their mothers and the boys up in the hay loft."[12]

There would be rides in the enormous sleigh that was named the Julia Dean, after the famous actress Julia Dean Hayne. The gracefully curved sides were painted green, and the huge box, filled with buffalo robes and hay, could accommodate fifty children of various sizes.

As Lucy observed and participated in the amazingly warm, secure, and fascinating lives her daughters enjoyed, she must often have thought back to the decision of her youth, knowing surely that the Lord had guided her to this time and place.

After a year Lucy returned to the Lion House, for she was pregnant with her third daughter, who was born on February 22, 1863. Lucy named the baby Rhoda Mabel, Rhoda being the name of Brigham's sister. Now, for a time, she had the luxury of caring for her baby and enjoying her two older children.

But life in the family was always a round of serving, learning, and carrying your share. There were always things to be done and challenges to meet, and many of these centered around the subject of education.

At this time Brigham had engaged a French teacher and a shorthand professor, thus supplementing the regular school curriculum, for a new schoolhouse had been built in 1862. This freed up the large room on the northwest side of the basement in the Lion House, which was now turned over to Lucy's care. What did she choose to do with it? She made it a haven for young people, where they could gather to talk and visit together, and do simple things such as pulling molasses candy or popping corn. She understood, and was trusted, and many good times were enjoyed there, including the performance of delightful theatricals, using the raised platform which their father had constructed there, a makeshift theatre which thrilled their hearts.

A small room led off from the large one, and so Lucy fixed it up as a warm little bedroom for her mother's visits, or for the use of anyone who came to visit, and was in need of a place to stay.

In her biography of her father Susa wrote, "Brigham Young loved knowledge and truth better than he loved his own life."[13]

Brigham taught, "The principle of intelligence is within us. . . . The principle is inherent, in the organization of all intelligent beings, so that we are capable of receiving, and receiving, and receiving, from the inexhaustible fountain of knowledge and truth."[14]

And again, "No person possesses intelligence, in any degree, that he has not received from the God of heaven, or, in other words, from the Fountain of all intelligence, whether he acknowledges his God in it or not."[15]

Education was of key importance to Brigham, and six years after the Lion House was completed he built a large schoolhouse for his children, with educational ideas of his own in mind. The windows, as Susa explained, were built high "so that the light should not fall directly on the pupil's eyes. The benches and desks were unique. We sat on benches or wooden chairs . . . exactly fitted to our backs and legs so that we suffered no discomfort by having to hang our feet or to stoop over the desk. Each child had a separate desk with sloping lid and place for ink bottles in the corner."[16]

That Brigham's views were enlightened is further indicated by his prescribed schedule for the day. "School opened at 9 o'clock and was dismissed at 4 p.m., with a dinner interval from 12 to 1:30. In the morning there was a recess of an hour and another half hour diversion in the afternoon How delightful were those breaks!"[17]

A balanced schedule of school, work, and play allowed Brigham Young's children to love learning, love structure, and to feel good about themselves and about the world around them.

Harriet Cook had taught the children in the Lion House and continued once the school was built. Neighbor children were also welcomed to come to the school, if interested. Born in Oneida County, New York, she became the fourth wife of Brigham Young in 1843. Harriet came to the Valley in 1848, and her father, though a devoted member of the Quaker faith, gave her five hundred dollars in gold! She possessed many outstanding qualities and skills, and was an especially excellent cook. She was also an accomplished enough seamstress that she worked for a time at the ZCMI store.

Karl G. Maeser was a distinguished convert from Germany, bringing a superior background in education with him but finding no outlet for his gifts among the Saints in the Valley, who were still struggling to feed and take care of their families. Though Brigham appointed him head of the Union Academy, his conditions only marginally improved. Coming from a noble line of brilliant, successful educators, he now found himself reduced to going round the neighborhoods with his wheelbarrow, asking with all humility for what assistance others might be willing to provide.

In 1864 Brigham Young stepped in and appointed him private tutor to his children. Ellis Shipp, who profited greatly from this association during her years living in the Beehive House, wrote: "As a pupil of Professor Maeser how blessed was my life! Every moment in his presence seemed a benediction, so great was his spiritual influence, his intuitive uplift to all that was pure and divine. He was by nature spiritualistic. His implicit faith in *The Living God* was an integral part of his being. . . . I realized a truly great blessing in sharing the immensity of his knowledge, his power to impart the wealth of his intelligence and superior wisdom."[18]

All this was happening around her, and Lucy was in the midst of it. One of the passions that was beginning to emerge within her was a common one in this large Young household: the love of music, the need of music in daily life. Brigham had secured David Evans, and several teachers after him, to give music lessons to any of his children who desired them. There were three organs and two pianos in the family, just to start with. Susa wrote with happy assurance: "Brigham Young's whole family were musical and he was happy when he could sit at ease in his own prayer-room surrounded by his wives and children, listening to the songs of Zion sung by the tuneful voices of sons and daughters. Some of his favorite sentimental songs were 'My Old Kentucky Home,' and 'Sweet Nellie Gray.'"[19]

There were several notable bands in the Valley boasting stringed and brass instruments, and several pianos had been brought across the plains. The leader of the Nauvoo Brass Band was an English convert, William Pitt. He "brought vast stores of music with him which served as the basis of later collections. Instruments were also imported from England."[20]

Very sophisticated classical music was performed in the Salt Lake Theatre, including Handel's oratorio, *The Messiah*. Colonel Kane's perception and praise are worth recording here: "Well as I knew the peculiar fondness of the 'Mormons' for music, their orchestra astonished me by its numbers and fine drill. The story was that an eloquent Mormon missionary had converted its members in a body at an English town, and that they took up their trumpets, trombones, drums, and hautboys together, and followed him to America. . . . When the battalion was enlisted, some of the performers were to accompany it; but they all refused. Their fortunes went with the Camp of the Tabernacle. They had led the Farewell Service in the Nauvoo Temple. Their office now was to guide the monster choruses and Sunday hymns . . . 'for the calling of the assembly, and for the journeying of the camp,' to knoll the people into church."[21]

Lucy loved music with much the same passion as her husband. She began by taking music lessons, then by teaching music to the children of some of their closest friends: the Kimballs, the Whitneys, the Wells. At length Brigham discovered the underlying purpose or scheme: they were saving money to purchase an organ, and either Lucy, or her daughter Dora, seemed to be constantly giving lessons or practicing themselves in order to obtain their goal. One of Lucy's dearest friends was Helen Mar Whitney, who was mother to Orson Whitney, who was, himself, a gifted musician and member of the Salt Lake Theatre orchestra.

As subtly as he could, Brigham came to their aid "just adding enough to their savings to put the organ at once within their reach."[22]

In all things Lucy partook of the spirit of self-sufficiency. She was curious but at the same time trusting, and when new things came along for her mind to figure out and her hands to do, she was always willing to try.

One of these new things was a Wheeler and Wilcox sewing machine. Lucy and the other sister wives suddenly found one in their possession! Lucy not only sewed curtains for the Green Room but also the first large carpet for the stage.

The following story gives great insight into the way Lucy "worked," the way she tackled the challenges of her life. Susa writes: "Father was always solicitous to save his wives extra steps . . . every new machine, domestic gadget . . . father bought . . About the year 1868, knitting machines found their way west and father bought a number of them and installed them in one of the Lion House rooms. He thought his dear wives would be glad to throw away their knitting needles. . . .

"Who wanted to tinker with the complicated popping keys and threads on those treadle contraptions? One after another refused, but when he asked Mother, she flew to the task, and he allowed her to hire three emigrant sisters who helped her to set up a real domestic knitting factory in the Lion House. . . . Stockings were whizzed off, socks ticked on, comforters slid through the noisy machines, and the foundation stones of our present Utah knitting factories were laid in that happy, busy sitting room."[23]

Life never held still and Lucy was happy, as always, to be busy doing something useful, and helpful to others.

NOTES

1. Gates, "From Impulsive Girl to Patient Wife: Lucy Bigelow Young," 5.
2. Clarissa Young Spencer, and Mabel Harmer, *Brigham Young at Home* (Salt Lake City: Deseret Book, 1972), 147.
3. Gates and Widtsoe, *Life of Brigham Young*, 81–82.
4. *Journal of Discourses*, volume 1, 30.
5. Gates, ibid., 5.
6. Gates and Widtsoe, *Life of Brigham Young*, 263.
7. Lee Davidson, "Camp Floyd," *Deseret News*, October 28, 2005.
8. Ibid.
9. McCloud, *Personal Portrait*, 209.
10. Whitley, *Brigham Young Homes*, 154.
11. Ibid., 57.
12. Gates and Widtsoe, *Life Story*, 343.
13. Ibid., 299.
14. Widtsoe, *Discourses of Brigham Young*, 94.

15. Ibid., 148.
16. Gates and Widtsoe, *Life Story*, 346.
17. Ibid., 249.
18. McCloud, *Not In Vain*, 55.
19. Ibid.
20. Gates and Widtsoe, *Life Story*, 249.
21. Ibid., 242–43.
22. Gates, *Impetuous Girl*, 6.
23. Ibid., 7.

Chapter Four

We have no knowledge of how it came to pass, but in 1867 or 1868 Lucy adopted a child, the same age as Mabel, who would have been four to five years old. There was a Sister MacMahon in the Valley who was a full-blooded East Indian woman, born to the upper classes and married to an English officer, Arthur MacMahon, who apostatized while the little family still lived in Calcutta. Yet Sister MacMahon was faithful, and the little branch there was known to have often held their meetings in her home.

The little girl was named Indiana Mary Maybert, though she was known as Ina to the family in the Lion House. Her parents had died in India, and her grandmother died not too long after her arrival in Salt Lake City in 1865. Lucy never did have enough children to satisfy her heart and welcomed this little one with open arms, enjoying seeing the two small girls, so much the same age and size, romping through the early days of childhood together.

Susa, in the account of her mother's life, says only that Ina married a son of James Jack, who was Brigham's "trusted private clerk, and she died at the early age of nineteen years old."[1] In a *Times and Seasons* online article by Ardis F. Parshall in 2007, new research seems to have indicated that Indiana took her own life when she was just seventeen. Whatever the case, Ina's young life was cut short, and Lucy must have deeply grieved.

Shortly after this time, as the two little girls were growing up together, a trouble of grievous proportions emerged. Eudora, or Dora as she was called, was Lucy's eldest daughter, and she was falling in love with a young man of a cheery disposition and a handsome face, named Frank Morley Dunford. His people were all converts to the Church, but somewhere along the way he had inherited or somehow developed "a deadly weakness of will and lack of self-control. He drank."[2]

Brigham took immediate action and sent his daughter to school in Provo at the Utah University branch there. But when she returned she was convinced that she was more in love than ever.

Some decisive action needed to be taken. He proposed the idea of sending Lucy and her girls to Saint George in southern Utah, where the climate was mild and warm year round, and he liked the idea of spending his winters there, since he had begun to suffer greatly from rheumatism. This ought to remove Dora far enough away!

Brigham had actually concluded definite plans to spend his winters in St. George and to spur the progress of building a temple there. He had thus chosen two wives to pick up and move to St George at his request: Lucy and Eliza Burgess, who both "seemed content to live in the background. Each woman was in her early forties and both had teenaged children. Eliza's seventeen-year-old son probably stayed in Salt Lake City where he worked for the *Deseret News* as a telegraph operator."[3]

But it did not prove to be so. In the busyness of preparing and packing for the St. George move, Brigham arranged for both Lucy and Susa to take instruction at the new Golightly Bakery in bread-making and cake-making, and in the finer art of candy-making. And Dora, left too much to her own devices, was making plans of her own.

In the midst of all of this Dora made and carried out her own desires. The somewhat cruel aspect existed in the timing: 3 October, 1870—Lucy's fortieth birthday. And in the happy confusion of a party being held in her honor, Dora slipped out and married her sweetheart, Morely Dunford, secretly—*with* the aid of her sister, Susa! Susa acted as witness, while her sister was married by a Presbyterian minister! Why? Time and any writings on the matter give us no answers. She was young, still in her teens. She was creative and drawn in by the excitement. She was helping her sister. She did not share the mature and legitimate fears that her parents felt.

Lucy's feelings upon the discovery can only be imagined. The journey to St. George went forward—taking not hours, or the better part of a day—but, without the miracle of rails going that far south, the journey took fourteen days, and the roads were uncomfortably rough.

The red hills and the red-tinted sand at their feet, the bluffs and stunted cedar trees were very different from the loved home they had left behind. But Brigham had already seen to the building of mills, including one for cotton, shops for various commodities, and a great planting of fruit trees, from fig to apricot, as well as every kind of grape vine.

Lucy was delighted when she discovered that the house Brigham had prepared for her was in the old New England style, with a large front porch, long windows opening onto it, and large ample rooms indoors with a downstairs bedroom and three upstairs, and every luxury she could think of waiting in her kitchen.

The out-of-doors was just as impressive, with fruit trees, flowers, and grape vines, and a kindly English gardener to oversee it all. There were corrals and a large barn, with turkeys, chickens, and cows, which Lucy insisted on milking herself.

There are always some drawbacks, however, to the most idyllic of situations. Brigham did arrive for the winter, making the house crowded, for Brigham Jr. and his wife, Lizzie, also came to stay, and there were sleeping rooms required for the hired girls and men. Lucy and Brigham took the bedroom on the main level, and the children were allocated to sleeping on the floor!

It was actually good that things were so busy and home-like, for Lucy had been accustomed to living in the "thick of things," knowing of all the challenges, difficulties, and desires of the larger family around her for fifteen years. Perhaps it was with some relief that she turned to domestic tasks and worked at making Brigham and his visitors, as well as his family, feel well-cared for and at home. Now she could hone her own cooking and baking skills as well, and there was a gentle beauty in this place which, for all intents and purposes was hers alone.

With the coming of spring Lucy was able to go out of doors, work with the gardener, Sammy Gould, in her garden, and begin to make it her own. She dug deep into the knowledge and memories she carried with her. In Susa's words: "She drew all the New England traditions— and superstitions—about when to plant so as to catch the right time of the moon—as well as the exact spaces apart for carrot seeds to be planted and onion sprouts to be set."4

Remembering the extra work duties that Lucy had assumed of her own accord, such as milking and caring for her cows, she was now seriously inundated with the care of the workers and the care and entertainment of a consistent barrage of guests, such "entertainment" being a responsibility in itself.

Lucy's health was not as good as it should be, but her energies and desires to be "useful" had not flagged. The winters in St. George were relatively cool and mild, offsetting the weeks of summer where the temperatures would rise above 100 degrees. But there were no winter storms to curtail work and fellowshipping activities, and Lucy urged her daughters to become involved in the community, to use their gifts and experience to make a difference.

In every instance Lucy herself did the same, leading her girls by example in ways that were natural to her. Mary Chamberlain, in her life sketch, writing of her childhood in St. George, gives us priceless insights into Lucy and the consistent way in which she lived her life:

"One of my first teachers in Primary or Sunday School was Sister Lucy B. Young . . . among other things she taught us was that our Father in Heaven was real and tangible and that we should pray to him just like we would go to our earthly father and ask for whatever we wanted, but we must not feel badly if we did not get everything we prayed for, because it might not be for our good, so we should always say, 'Father, if it be right, grant me this desire,' or 'Thy will be done.'

"She explained the importance of partaking of the sacrament worthily. If we had done or said anything to injure another, it was our duty to go to them and make it right and ask their forgiveness and also to ask the Lord's forgiveness. If we would do this and then offer up a silent prayer as we partook of the emblems, asking for the Lord's spirit to be with us during the coming week, we would surely be blessed. Also that whenever we went to meeting, if we would offer up a silent prayer that something might be said for our particular benefit, we would never go away disappointed, no matter how humble or unlearned the speaker might be. These and many other teachings I remember."5

Change, constant change, and many new adjustments were becoming a large part of Lucy's life. But she could not yet conceive of the rare and joyous opportunities awaiting her.

It was a blow when Brigham told her of his determination to build a larger house, with room for a nice-sized office, a vineyard, and a garden. He was legitimately concerned about the strain on her, the demands of care and entertainment placed upon her. She should not have to sacrifice her home; never that. And he was arranging for his wife Amelia Folsom to come down the following winter—not alone, but bringing the help she would obviously need to care for him and handle the burden of entertainment.

This made sense, but not to the heart of a loving wife who, as Susa expressed it, "was human, was a woman!" But she quickly added: "But she was also a saint, and a converted Latter-day Saint, so she knew the principle of celestial and of plural marriage was true, and she had long ago learned her lessons. So, she just quietly made up her mind to meet the situation with her customary sweet patience and faith."[6]

Susa gives us some interesting insights into the beginnings, the inception, of the St. George Temple.

"The winters spent in sunny St. George were occupied in drafting out plans for building a House of the Lord. Brigham had his daughter, the writer, with him. She read over and over again to him the descriptions given in Leviticus of the Tabernacle in the wilderness and the account of Solomon's Temple as given in 1 and 2 Chronicles and 1 and 2 Kings. He must know just how long was a cubit; exactly where and how the baptismal font, called the sea of brass, stood; and all about the formation of the brazen oxen, upon which the font rested.

"He was familiar with the dimensions and construction of the Nauvoo Temple planned by the Prophet Joseph Smith. . . . He was determined that the font to be placed in the Temple (the only one he should build and see completed) should be as near those of Solomon's Temple as unhurried hands could make it, and with as perfect lines and comeliness as artists could design. He presented this baptismal font, which really was a work of art, as his personal contribution to the Temple."[7]

Surely no other person knew and loved, learned and served in the temple of the Lord more than Brother Brigham. During the last days of Nauvoo, many of the Saints worked long hours and sacrificed that as many as possible might receive their endowments before they turned their backs on the City of Joseph, the city they loved, and went forward, with only faith to guide them, literally into the unknown.

But Brigham, even after he told the people that they must close the temple and leave or their enemies would be upon them, took compassion and stayed, performing endowments for an additional week. His journal reflected his dedication in statements such as these: "I officiated in the Temple until midnight. . . . "Officiated in the temple during the night until three-thirty a.m. . . . Tarried in the temple all night. . . . I have given myself up entirely to the work of the Lord in the Temple night and day, not taking more than four hours sleep, upon an average, per day, and going home but once a week."[8]

Susa also added: "The large Bible he (Brigham) used is full of notes on the margins, made by himself and his daughter. He left within its covers his own rough draft of the lower floor plan of the building and it shows exactly how he shaped out matters for architects to develop to perfection."[9]

The temple site was dedicated November 9, 1871. Built by tithing and other free-will offerings, the edifice cost more than $100,000. The three-day formal dedication took place in April of 1877. Brigham had spent what was to be his last winter in instructing, training, and assisting so that all was in keeping in what the Prophet Joseph had taught him.

But in the midst of these wonderful and momentous plans and events, family life continued with challenges and problems in plenty.

In December of 1872 Susa married a cousin of Dora's husband. Whatever possessed her? He was a little older, a trained dentist. Perhaps she felt, or at least hoped, there would be more solidarity there. But, as Susa confided, "He, too, drank, and the marriage was a most unfortunate one, only that it gave Susa two fine children."[10] For a time both Susa and Dora lived with their husbands in Salt Lake, and Lucy's mother spent the winter of 1874–75 with her daughter in St. George.

Brigham's heart was one of loving and forgiving, of sorrowing and helping, more than most people realized. In a letter written to Lucy in June of 1875 he said: "Dora and Susa expect to be sick in August . . . (this was the accepted, a bit more subtle way of saying that their babies were due to be born at that time). . . . If you would like to come here and bring Mabel with you and stay during their sickness, I will be much pleased to have you do so. . . . Leave your mother to take charge of the house and things."[11]

So, Lucy had the pleasure of nursing both of her daughters during their confinements, remaining many weeks, until the early fall. And at that same autumn time Susa also moved back to St. George.

The overriding vision—the eternal vision filled with power and fueled with love—was constantly before Brigham's eyes. In a speech to the people, recorded in the *Journal of Discourses*, he made this clear: "We are trying to save the living and the dead. The living can have their choice, the dead have not. Millions of them died without the Gospel, without the Priesthood, and without the opportunities that we enjoy. We shall go forth in the name of Israel's God and attend to the ordinances for them. And through the Millennium, the thousand years that the people will love and serve God, we will build temples and officiate therein for those who have slept for hundreds and thousands of years—those who would have received the truth if they had had the opportunity; and we will bring them up, and form the chain entire, back to Adam."[12]

Brigham arranged for the April general conference of the Church to be held in St. George and, in connection with this, the formal dedicatory services of the temple. The prophet gave instruction after instruction, especially concerning the uses and magnification of the Priesthood, and explained again and again the important details of the ordinances of the temple.

He, himself, spent a good deal of his time performing the work for his parents and other of his kindred dead. Five of his daughters, a son, and a nephew were privileged to be with him in the effort. Wilford

Woodruff, who would be the first president of this, the first temple, "baptized Susie (Susa) for one of her deceased friends, *the first baptism for the dead in the St. George temple.* Afterward, Wilford and Brigham laid their hands on Susie's head and confirmed her on the deceased's behalf."[13]

He was obviously happy to have this daughter back with him, at his side, one with his own desires and spiritual aims. He understood, and it was certain that he watched her sorrows, efforts, and struggles.

Susa knew this. She had been well taught by example from both her parents, as well as by precept. She taught them: "Keep your troubles to yourself, in the sacred privacy of your own bosom."[14] Eliza R. Snow had re-enforced it.

"Never tell any body if you are sick or sorry. Don't make others weary with your complainings."[15]

"Indeed, Susa had seen Brigham's wives exercise this high level of control. Writing about the quality years later, as editor of the *Young Woman's Journal,* she told the girls of the Church: 'Words are the weakest as well as the strongest things on earth. They are weak when they betray our spirits, and they are strong when they obey an intelligent will."[16]

It was already well known among friends and family that Lucy possessed the gift of healing. "Eventually she became widely known for her ability to treat many ills with herbs and blessings, including blessings using consecrated oil."[17]

Lucy "was appointed as President of all the Sister Workers in the Temple. Imagine, if you can, the joy and divine gratitude which sang in her soul!"[18]

She knew in her heart that her work was here. She had already been helping, lending her wisdom and grace, even to the details of the drapes and curtains and how they were to be hung. She knew she was capable of serving the Lord honorably in his House. She knew also the only manner in which she could accomplish it, and that was with His help, His guidance, His strengthening affirmation and power. She needed to be a worthy instrument in His hands. And it is this, from the very beginning, to which she dedicated her efforts and her heart.

Dora left her husband and returned to St. George so that all three of Lucy's daughters were there together. Both she and Susa were chosen as ordinance workers, Susa also serving as the assistant recorder.

Lucy had never been a leader, or considered herself a leader like some of her sister-wives, such as Eliza R. Snow and Zina. But as Susa understood and eulogized, "No wonder Mother felt as if she were having a foretaste of heaven!"[19]

NOTES

1.   Gates, "From Impulsive Girl to Patient Wife: Lucy Bigelow Young," 7.
2.   Ibid.
3.   Ibid.
4.   Ibid.
5.   Richard E. Turley and Brittany A. Chapman, *Women of Faith in the Latter Days*, volume 3 (Salt Lake City: Deseret Book, 2014). See also Janelle M. Higbee, *Mary Elizabeth Woolley Chamberlain: A Strong and Abiding Faith*, 29–30.
6.   Gates, "From Impulsive Girl to Patient Wife: Lucy Bigelow Young," 9.
7.   Gates, *Life Story*, 234–34.
8.   Susan Evans McCloud, *Personal Portrait*, 130.
9.   Gates, *Life Story*, 225.
10. Gates, "From Impulsive Girl to Patient Wife: Lucy Bigelow Young,"14.
11. Ibid.
12. *Journal of Discourses*, volume 14, 77.
13. *Saints, Volume 2: No Unhallowed Hand*, 427.
14. Barbara B. Smith and Blythe Darlyn Thatcher, editors, *Heroines of the Restoration* (Salt Lake City: Bookcraft, 1997), 234.
15. Ibid.
16. McCloud, *Power of Susa Young Gates*, 234.
17. Colleen Whitley, *Brigham Young's Homes*, 206.
18. Gates, "From Impulsive Girl to Patient Wife: Lucy Bigelow Young," 15.
19. Ibid.

Chapter Five

Everything done in the St. George Temple was done for the first time. Nauvoo had been somewhat different, and everything done there was done in a setting of poverty, extremity, and fear. Now patterns would be set and standards established. Lucy quietly went about creating her own, praying with all of her heart, all of the energies of her soul, that the blessings she desired for herself and for those she served might be granted.

Lucy lived in a state of prayer, and in the quiet humility that comes from an assurance that the Lord will magnify you as well as aid you when you are serving His purposes in His holy house.

Fasting also became a consistent part of her life. She knew the edge of power, spiritual awareness, and readiness that it alone can lend. The line in our well-loved hymn expresses it: "I would be my brother's keeper, I would learn the healer's art."[1] This was Lucy's gift, the use of which she honed and perfected day following day.

Speaking of her mother, Susa wrote: "Her future life on the earth, for she was then just forty-seven years old, lay along true spiritual lines. This was emphasized for her when she had her last—her very last—visit with Father, in St. George. . . . He was to start for Salt Lake the next morning and he was solicitous to learn if she had everything for her comfort and well being."[2]

It is easy to perceive that all elements in their relationship, everything between them, was nourished and solidified in this last time they were to share their mortal experience together. Brigham nourished those he loved, nourished his people, because he lived by the heart, by the Spirit, as well as by reason and the mind. He spared no words when talking of marriage to the Saints: "I will tell you here, now, in the presence of the Almighty god, it is not the privilege of any Elder to have even one wife, before he has honored his Priesthood, before he has magnified his calling. If you obtain one, it is by mere permission, to see what you will do, how you will act, whether you will conduct yourself in righteousness in that holy estate."[3]

Brigham's mortal powers were constantly being enlightened by the eternal powers that guided him, so that his understanding drove deep, as he labored to teach his people those sacred truths which his soul embraced. In a consummate sermon on marriage, he told his listeners:

"But the whole subject of the marriage relation is not in my reach, nor in any other man's reach on this earth. It is without beginning of days or end of years; it is a hard matter to reach. We can tell some things with regard to it; it lays the foundation for worlds, for angels, and for the Gods; for intelligent beings to be crowned with glory, immortality, and eternal lives. In fact, it is the thread which runs from the beginning to the end of the holy Gospel of Salvation—of the Gospel of the Son of God; it is from eternity to eternity."[4]

All Lucy held in her heart from her last moments with her husband, all the sanctification she would endure in the next few days and weeks at his sudden death and the loss of him—all this was part of the purification that fitted her for the work which she had been called to do.

In the last week of August 1877, a dreaded telegram brought them word that Brigham Young was ill and dying. Susa was already in the north, so Lucy left St. George, accompanied by her daughter Mabel and under the tender care of President Woodruff, in a simple and not incredibly comfortable buckboard wagon. Word was consistently sent ahead for fresh horses and rested drivers, for they traveled without stops, all through the silent nights, leaving on a Wednesday morning and reaching Milford on Saturday night. From there they could take the railroad to Salt Lake Sunday morning—and, therefore, Lucy arrived, beleaguered, her senses blurred, one slender hour before the funeral services for her husband were to begin.

Brigham's death was sudden and unexpected. He had just turned seventy-six years old on June 1, 1877, and had traveled to reorganize the Box Elder Stake on August 19. After prayers on August 23, he retired early, then awoke later in great pain from what was, at length, correctly diagnosed as a ruptured appendix. He suffered greatly but cheerfully. When he was removed from his bed in the Lion House and placed by the open window, "he seemed to partially revive, and opening his eyes, he gazed upward, exclaiming 'Joseph! Joseph! Joseph!' and the divine look in his face seemed to intimate that he was communicating with his beloved friend, Joseph Smith, the Prophet. This name was the last word he uttered."[5]

Brigham's body was taken from the Beehive House to the tabernacle on September 1, and more than 25,000 Saints filed by to pay their last respects. The following day, the Sabbath, the funeral services were held in the tabernacle, with more than twelve thousand people somehow cramming in to the limited space. Joseph Daynes had composed a special funeral march for Brigham Young, and George Careless led a 225-voice choir in singing several appropriate songs.

Four thousand people marched eight abreast to the small family burial spot a little above the Lion and Beehive houses. There was no pomp and ceremony, and no one was dressed in black. But the stunned sense of loss and of humility attended the grieving crowd.

Despite wild ideas and conjecturing, would Brother Brigham have left anything out of order? After Congress passed a disincorporating act against the Church, limiting its holdings to $50,000, church properties were placed in the hands of the president and other trustworthy leaders to administer. After Brigham's death the auditing committee, "going back to the very beginning of accounts in the Salt Lake Valley," found them "strictly correct" with "very slight exceptions" and were impressed with "the accuracy of his accounts."[6]

He had been just as thorough and fair with his family. Susa explained:

"The will was a model of equity and justice. Each wife was provided with a home of her own or a life-suite in the Lion House, with ample provision for maintenance in comfort to the end of her days. Each daughter . . . inherited equally with the boys and each other; each also had a building lot given them in the Upper Garden. . . a fair monthly income was to be paid to the mothers until the property was settled up, when they were to receive an increased amount, according to the increased values of the property."[7]

Brigham Young always stressed love and the power of personal revelation: "I would place first and foremost the duty of seeking unto the Lord our God until we open the path of communication from heaven to earth—from God to our own souls."[8]

Brigham Young had no illusions. He often said that he was no more important than any other member of the Church. He urged a Christ-like awareness of one another in these tender words: "God bless the humble and the righteous, and may He have compassion upon us because of the weakness that is in our nature. And considering the great weakness and ignorance of mortals, let us have mercy upon each other."[9]

What myriad of memories and emotions must have coursed through Lucy's mind upon that day and in the days that followed. She grew up under the gentle touch of his powerful intellect and his tender, ever-patient heart. He taught her much—partly because she was so willing to grow and learn. His family, and even his people, held testimony of the fact that interwoven with the terrible majesty of his own powers, of his faith, of the desires that drove him to care for the small, insignificant one as well as for the whole—Brigham *understood*, and he never lost sight of the One who held the reigns, who set the compass, and guided the ship.

Let these words of his serve as a last witness and testament of Brigham Young's, which no one can doubt or belie:

"What earthly power can gather a people as this people have been gathered, and hold them together as this people have been held together? It is not Brigham, it was not Joseph, nor Heber, nor any of the rest of the Twelve . . . but it is the Lord God Almighty that holds this people together, and no other power."[10]

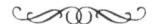

As supervisor of the sister workers in the St. George Temple, Lucy trained them, loved them, and inspired them. When Wilford Woodruff had his vision, as recorded in his Journal on August 21,

1877, a rare and most sacred opportunity came to Lucy Bigelow Young. As President Woodruff declared on April 9, 1898, "The Spirits of the dead gathered around me, wanting to know why we did not redeem them. Said they, 'You have had the use of the Endowment House for a number of years, and yet nothing has ever been done for us. We laid the foundation of the government you now enjoy, and we never apostatized from it, but we remained true to it and were faithful to God.'

"Everyone of those men that signed the Constitution of Independence with others, including General Washington, called upon me as an Apostle of the Lord Jesus Christ, in the Temple at St. George, two consecutive nights, and demanded at my hands that I should go forth and attend to the ordinances of the House of God for them."[11]

He did so, enlisting the assistance of Brother McCallister, until he had been baptized for one hundred names, and had baptized his companion for an additional twenty-one.

Wilford Woodruff further stated, "Sister Lucy Bigelow Young went forth into the font and was baptized for Martha Washington and her family and 70 of the 'eminent women' of the world."[12]

There were actually eleven women in the Washington line, including Christiane von Goethe; Charlotte von Schiller; Charlotte, Sir Walter Scott's wife; Sarah Ford, the mother of Samuel Johnson; Isabella, the wife of Thackeray; Anna Isabella, the wife of Lord Byron; Jean Armour, the wife of Robert Burns; William Wordsworth's wife, Mary Hutchinson; both the wife and the mother of Daniel Webster; and sweet young Mathilda Hoffman, who was betrothed to the gentle writer Washington Irving and died at the age of seventeen, before they could be wed.

Most surely, Lucy felt the spirits of some of these women as she performed the sacred ordinances on their behalf. Martha Washington, for instance, was born to a wealthy family and given every advantage of education and training which women of that time could receive, which included learning how to read and write. At nineteen she married her first husband, Daniel Parke Custis, and they had four children but only two survived. Upon his death she married George Washington and, though they never had children of their own, he was a gentle, devoted father to her son and daughter. Sadly, Patsy died at the age of seventeen, and Jack died while serving with Washington in the war.

Martha set the standard with her kindness, care, and courage. She spent every winter of the war in camp with her husband, and raised money to lessen the grim suffering of the soldiers there. She encouraged their faltering spirits and listened patiently to the fears and hardships of the wives, as well. She gave her life to this sacred emerging country, as much as her husband did.

So the temple days progressed. And through faith, continual prayer, and fasting, the powers of Lucy's spirit were magnified by the Lord and molded and finely honed to a perfection that enabled her to accomplish a mighty work.

Women would come to Lucy seeking aid for many ailments. There is the accounting in the *Young Woman's Journal* in October of 1892 of a sister who had not walked for twelve years and was brought to Lucy: "Under the cheering faith of Sister Young she went through the day's ordinance and was perfectly healed of her affliction."[13]

The majority of women who came to her were coming in hope, or an almost hopelessness, being unable to conceive and have the children their hearts desired. In the sketch of Lucy's life this is tenderly described: "Numbers of these childless women have sought out the prayers and faith of Sister Young in her temple duties, and have afterwards returned, as Hannah of old, to bring up their promised child to receive further blessings in the temple.

"Volumes would not contain the myriad instances of cases of illness and disease healed by the power of God under Sister Young's hands. . . . When her hands are upon the head of another in blessing, the words of inspiration and personal prophecy that flow from her lips are like a stream of living fire."[14]

When the Logan Utah Temple was ready to be opened to the Saints in May of 1884, Lucy was chosen to assist in training the workers for the ordinances that would be performed in this holy place, this second temple to be built in the land of Deseret. She was happy to do so, but when the work was well established and under way, she returned to her temple, and her home, in St. George

Again, when the Manti Utah Temple was to be dedicated by Wilford Woodruff in May of 1888, Lucy's services were required. Perhaps she remembered the time in April of 1877, just months before Brigham Young's death, when he dedicated the site for this third temple—determined the site, really, for no one had thought of building there before. In the morning of that day, April 25, he had asked Brother Warren S. Snow to go with him to what would be the southeast corner of the temple site, and told him, "Here is the spot where the Prophet Moroni stood and dedicated this piece of land for a Temple site, and that is the reason why the location is made here, and we can't move it from this spot."[15]

From the sketch of Lucy's life in *The Young Woman's Journal* we read these tender words: "There she was at the dedication of that temple, and many and glorious were the manifestations which were given to her in that beautiful time. She remained here some months in charge of the work until Sister M. W. Snow could come and take up that labor. Again she returned to her work in the St. George Temple."[16]

While these very significant experiences were taking place for Lucy, life all about her was going on its way. Dora had married again, and Susa was what she called "a grass-widow," for she finally divorced her husband in 1878. She had been but sixteen when she married him, and the marriage survived for five years. Her daughter, Leah, and her son, Bailey, were her biggest concern right now. She had gained custody of her little son, but her precious daughter was snatched away from her, far enough distant that she had little means of communicating with her at all.

But Lucy was there once more to encourage and uphold her daughter. Her own mother sorrow she kept carefully in her bosom, as Brigham and Eliza R. Snow had both always gently admonished. The temple work was a spiritual mainstay, she knew, for Susa as well as for herself.

In 1878 Susa found her way to the Brigham Young University in Provo, where President Maeser, her beloved professor from girlhood days, welcomed her and advised her on what to do with her life.

Susa could never hold still, and an opportunity right before her eyes was impossible to ignore! She organized the music department of the school and added her support and expertise to everything she touched, organizing the Academy Choir, who enthusiastically "learned ten choruses and anthems in two weeks. I am obliged to sing each part with everyone as I did in the old club. It is indeed *very* wearing on the lungs and nerves. But I love it, and am so glad I can assist the fresh young, and oftentimes sweet singers of Zion to praise God in melody and in song.

"During the Conference here we sang for the Twelve, and Bros. [John] Taylor, [Daniel H.] Wells, [Brigham] Young Jr., and [George F.] Gibbs expressed themselves highly pleased with our music. Both Bro. Taylor and Sister [Eliza R.] Snow expressed the very kindest feelings to me, and seemed to feel a great interest in my course."[17]

During this period her younger sister, Rhoda, was with her throughout the winter months. Susa, born in 1856 and Rhoda in 1863, were separated by seven years, so it was a case of the big sister taking the younger under her wing. Susa wrote often to her mother, and Lucy was able to share in the smallest details of their lives and to be encouraged by the growth Susa was sustaining.

This, from a letter of April 4, 1879, is characteristic: "Mother dear, I do not love any one on earth as well as my precious good Mother, except my little children. . . . I am happy, or at least as happy as mortals who have scared hearts and some memories can ever expect to be. In short, I am busy, contented, and useful. I am only twenty-three, so there is plenty of time, yes years and years of it for me yet. Let your heart be at rest for me, as long as I am in the Academy, I am safe. That is as long as I am a partaker of the spirit that rules in these walls, I am all right."[18]

The exchange of letters was a spiritual and satisfying union, very cherished by Lucy. Susa praises her sweet little son and tells her mother, "I write simple little letters to my precious 'little forsaken,' every little while"—referring to her daughter Leah, who was not permitted to be with her—"and thus keep my memory fresh in her mind. I always tell her to pray for the time when she will be with Mama again. She is well."[19]

It was easy for Lucy to see, and be deeply pleased, with the real influence which Brigham Young still exerted upon the mind and spirit of his daughter, even from beyond the grave. Susa was growing and deeply defining what she was, what she desired, and what she most wanted to become in life. Later in the month, in that same year of 1879, Susa, frustrated as being lumped in with her sister Dora, and considered to be worldly and untrue, wrote with a noticeable vehemence: "You do not seem to understand me or my purposes. Is it wrong to want to help build up God's Kingdom? The only desire I know of at present or at any time, is to live so that father will meet and welcome me."[20]

Susa's interactions with the apostles and the beloved Eliza R. Snow drew her thoughts and desires toward the father she so deeply missed. The words she wrote to Lucy are among the greatest tribute paid to that tender remarkable man. Rather than worrying that Brigham would be angry or cool due to his disappointment in her—for she had divorced her husband shortly after Brigham's death—Susa in June of the same year wrote:

"God help me to be worthy of the good opinion of all of the true Saints. For verily I want to be as near what father would wish me to be as it is possible for my weak, queer disposition to be. Oh Mother, don't you long to see father, to clasp his arms around your neck and hear his blessed voice pronounce those sweet words 'Welcome, my beloved, to your home.' Oh I know I am young and have a destiny in this Church to fulfill, but how I would love to go to father!"[21]

Lucy understood. She knew Susa's gifts and the depth of her dedication would help her to fulfill these desires. And she must have contemplated the somewhat strange facts that Brigham had acted in much the same capacity with her in the beginning: teaching her, lifting her, opening up the eyes of her understanding, and the founts of her yet untapped strengths. Then, as the unfolding blossomed more and more into reality, she came to know him as the most loving and caring of husbands, in whom she felt free to entrust all her difficulties and fears, all her spiritual desires and goals. He was the light both she and Susa had followed in gratitude, trust, and love.

NOTES

1. Susan Evans McCloud, "Lord, I Would Follow Thee," *Hymns of The Church of Jesus Christ of Latter-day Saints,* 220.

2. Gates, "From Impulsive Girl to Patient Wife: Lucy Bigelow Young," 15.

3. *Journal of Discourses,* volume 1, 119.

4. Ibid., volume 2, 90.

5. Susa Young, *Life Story,* 362.

6. Susan Evans McCloud, *Personal Portrait,* 386.

7. Ibid., 286.

8. *Journal of Discourses,* volume 8, 339.

9. Ibid., volume 10, 158.

10. Ibid., volume 10, 305.

11. April 10, 1898, General Conference Report: "Discourses of Wilford Woodruff," 160–61.

12. Ibid.

13. "Sketch of Sister Lucy B. Young in the Temples," *Young Woman's Journal,* volume 4, October 1892, 299.

14. Ibid.

15. www.churchofjesuschrist.rg/study/ensign/1978/03/the-manti-temple-?lang

16. *Young Woman's Journal,* volume 4, 299–300.

17. Kenneth W. Godfrey, M. Derr Godfrey, and Jill Mulway, *Women's Voices: An Untold History of the Latter-day Saints, 1830–1900* (Salt Lake City: Deseret Book, 1982), 335–36.

18. Ibid., 331.

19. Ibid.

20. Ibid., 333.

21. Ibid.

CHAPTER SIX

SUSA OFTEN CALLED ZINA, WHO WAS ONE OF BRIGHAM'S MORE WELL-known and accomplished wives, her "other mother." She had the opportunity to go with her now, at the end of her academy school term, on a rather exotic visit to the islands of Hawaii. She knew that her friend Jacob Gates would be there. She and Jacob, neighbors and acquaintances from St. George, had been corresponding on very friendly, perhaps even hopeful, terms. Susa felt at ease with him, able to converse openly, sharing her spirit and her mind—enough so that she wrote in one letter: "God is good, and He will help me to pick up the shattered threads of life and mend them into something useful."[1]

Therefore, Susa encouraged her mother to go east in the summer of 1880 in an effort to find and meet family members, discover information and copy records that she might bring back with her, and perform temple rites for.

Susa knew her mother's frugality and that she had sufficient money for such a worthwhile endeavor. She encouraged her mother to go by reminding that her own interest "in the phases of Temple work was almost comparable" to Lucy's own.[2]

Susa married Jacob on January 1, 1880, and they lived in St. George, very close to where her mother lived. The journey was very worthwhile for Lucy. New England spoke to her roots, and she was struck with how different her life was in the deserts of Utah than what she had known before.

In 1880, during the autumn following her family tour, Lucy celebrated her fiftieth birthday. She was still young, really, and had accomplished a number of remarkable things in her life. She knew that life was entering a phase of change, of new things happening in the lives of her children, of new, very different challenges for them all.

Among Lucy's challenges and uncertainties were the marriages of her two other daughters, Eudora in 1879 to Albert Hogan, and Rhoda the same year to Douglas McAllister. Both of these daughters bore sons first, though Dora's was to die very young.

Beyond this challenge was the fact that Dora was excommunicated from the Church in 1880. This would seem beyond belief to Lucy, despite all she must have known concerning her daughter's heart and the choices of her life. She continued on, laying her mother's grief at the feet of the Savior, which she had learned well how to do.

When Jacob Gates was called, suddenly and unexpectedly, on a mission to the Sandwich Islands, or Hawaii as we know it, he and Susa had been married for several years and were living in Provo, raising three children as well as Bailey, Susa's son. The whole situation surrounding the call was stressful from beginning to end, with confusion and last-minute changes, and the anguish of Susa's ex-husband, Alma Dunford, ignoring her letter requesting his agreement to her taking their son to Hawaii—only to show up at the last minute at the depot when they were preparing to depart! He brought a deputy with him, as well as a court order, which he smugly handed over. Susa could not take her son and had to leave a distressed and unhappy little boy behind.

Life in the islands was also a great challenge, especially since Susa was expecting another child when she began her life there. We know that Lucy went to stay with Susa and her little family in 1887. She came, and she helped, and her help was greatly needed! She employed that quiet, reassuring gift which had been hers since girlhood: she fit herself into every situation and every need. It is remembered that she liked being useful. She had learned, and learned again, that this gave life and purpose to all the trials and challenges which might otherwise come to seem almost pointless, with power to confuse, as well as to drag one down.

But here there was heartache and great suffering as well.

Susa had carved out a place for herself there. Jacob was working in a plant as a sugar bottler, as well as doing his missionary work. Most of what she did was woman's work, especially for her family. But she needed to cut and sew all the clothing they needed, as well: shirts and pants for Jacob and the boys and little dresses for their only daughter, six-year-old Lucy.

In February, her four-year-old son, Jay, showed signs of a fever and cough that kept growing worse. Susa had sat with him late into the night of the 22nd, and intended to fulfill the promise she had given to the suffering boy that she would not leave him.

But Jay seemed to be resting peacefully, and Jacob urged her to get some rest while he kept watch. Jay awoke and called and called for his mother, but Jacob, not knowing that the worst could happen, did not awaken her. Jay kept sinking, and as the afternoon waned, he died gently in his sleep.

Susa was inconsolable with grief and guilt. They were on a mission, the child along with them. How could such things happen now? Jacob was able to weep and mourn, but Susa was not. She also feared for the life of the baby that rested within her. And their ordeal was not over. Karl, only three years old, named after her beloved Karl G. Maeser, contracted the disease and died shortly after his brother.

Joseph F. Smith and his wife, Julina, were in Hawaii with the Gates. It was they who gently prepared the little bodies for burial. What their feelings must have been, remembering their beloved oldest daughter, Josephine, who had died at much the same age as these little boys.

Susa unburdened her heart to Lucy, before her mother had left to come and join her. She had at last felt again the stirrings of life in her womb, and she wrote: "A very faint motion comforts me with hope that life still beats under my saddened heart." She struggled to remember all the things she knew and believed, that this might stir up her much needed faith.

"With all this," she affirmed, "we know that God rules in the heavens. God has blessed me and helped me to bear my burdens. Praise His holy name forever."[3]

Lucy stayed in the islands long enough "to become [so] fluent in the Hawaiian language that she was able to share her testimony with the sisters there in their own language."[4] What an influence Lucy undoubtedly was upon the spiritually sensitive spirits of these Polynesian women. She had gone the extra mile, wanting to open her own heart to them and knowing that, in order to do so, she must speak in their tongue.

Lucy also had an opportunity that was precious to her: to meet Queen Lililuokalani and, with time and love, to become her true friend. The queen was in need of friends, and she drew people to her by the warmth and magnetism of her person. Lililuokalani was the last sovereign monarch of the Kingdom of Hawaii, and, despite the love of her people, this remarkable and powerful woman ruled for only three brief years. In 1898 the United States finally came off the victor in their determined efforts, and annexed the queen's beloved land as a U.S. territory.

Lucy's dear mother, Mary Gibb Bigelow, had been living with her in St. George and died there in April of 1888. She was seventy-eight years old, and it was a comfort to Lucy to know that she had been able to share these last years of her mother's mortal life before seeing her go on to be reunited with her husband.

Wives and husbands, husbands and wives . . . What an entanglement this had become in the lives of Lucy's daughters. Even Susa, the most solid of the three, had been divorced and was forced to do without her precious daughter and now, for a season, the raising of her son, as well.

Rhoda had married Daniel McCallister in 1879 and gave birth to one son. In 1888 she was married a second time to Brigham Will, and with him she also had a son. Lucy worried about her. This was a second husband; perhaps it would go better. And perhaps it was a blessing that the prayerful mother could not see into the future to the changes that would yet take place.

With Dora it was even worse; things with Dora were usually so. In 1879, the same year as Rhoda's first marriage, Dora married Albert Hogan, who was an already married attorney, and later a judge in Salt Lake. She bore and raised two children with Hogan, but her first son and her last daughter—named Lucy Mary after both her mother and her grandmother—died as infants.

In 1880 Dora was excommunicated from the Church. All the complications of this situation were not revealed, but she took legal action against the authority of the Church and against the executors of her father's estate. The claim could be guessed at: she accused them of defrauding the heirs of their inheritance.

Such things were usually left unwritten and were not even talked about in that time except with great care. Lucy kept in her heart the deep sorrow she felt for her eldest daughter, and she prayed, knowing the power of prayer was the greatest asset or help she possessed.

Three years following this difficult time, after returning from the Hawaiian mission, Susa accompanied her mother in a return to Worcester, Massachusetts, this time in order to attend a Bigelow family reunion. Perhaps Lucy's previous visit, and possible correspondence, had paved the way, for the mother and daughter were welcomed warmly and accepted as members of this large and notable New England family.

How many pathways must Lucy's mind have traveled during this time, back to the very extraordinary courtship of her mother by Nahum Bigelow, a man twenty-four years older than she, his absolute assurance that he wanted this girl to finish growing up and become his wife; the price they paid for their conversion to Mormonism, and the cruelties her father suffered when he was poisoned; the tender patience and faith of her young little mother as she tried to protect her children and to keep her husband alive. That little mother had died only two years before and sealed her earth life, her faithfulness, and her sacrifice as a vital, sacred part of her immortal existence. Lucy had always felt proud to be in the Bigelow family and to carry that heritage with her into the large, inclusive, diverse and dedicated family of Brigham Young.

There was growth everywhere, and new families constantly arrived to swell the ranks of the Saints in the Valleys of the Mountains. Change: the only constant in mortal life; and disappointment, which was the leavening ingredient requiring patience or, in a more spiritual sense, faith. Lucy had never harbored demanding, unrealistic expectations. Her purpose was to be useful unto the Lord, which meant serving His children and, in serving His children, expanding those powers which were like Him, which came through Him.

There was a definite closeness between Lucy and Susa; a sameness of interests, a oneness of purpose. Through Susa she was able to enjoy many exceptional experiences, not commonly offered to someone like herself.

In 1899 Susa and Lucy were invited to the International Council of Women in London, England. Susa had been a patron of the Council, but this was a special event to attend the first meeting of the Association in Europe, to go to London, *and* with every hope of having tea with the Queen!

This was an historic occasion. Lucy watched and listened carefully, realizing that leaders such as these around her were opening up a new world for women—both in the theatres of action which were now admitting them, as well as in the inner soul, the self of the woman, as she was emerging, growing, expanding, and discovering her own hidden reserves. At this time Council organizations existed in twenty-two countries, a significant growth from nine just ten years before, in 1888. The areas their efforts concentrated on were basic to life, not outlandish or unduly demanding. They included women in education, professional positions, social life, and even politics and industry.

Lucy had been born in an historic year—coming to earth in the year 1830 as the kingdom of God, under direction of the Savior, was breathing its first breaths of life as a new dispensation, after thousands of years of silence, and was being established to break down error and darkness so that the eternal in man might emerge. Was this women's movement under the direction of heaven as well? Good, noble women, brave and sacrificing, stood at its head. Years later Susa was to write in the *Relief Society Magazine*, "Woman's sphere hitherto confined expressly within the four walls of her home, was now to be limited by the confines of the Kingdom of God itself."[5]

If women of the Church could keep that at the center of their hearts, as the impetus of their actions, then yes, great things would happen under the care and direction of Heavenly Father. Lucy had lived and worked with Brigham Young. She knew the expansiveness of his knowledge and vision. Brigham had often taken positions and made statements supporting women's abilities in the workplace and in various aspects of community. Yet, there was a whole that was always stated or implied—not keeping woman "in her place" but providing safety, *and* the primary, unsurpassed influence, as this statement, explained by his daughter, Susa: "A measure of public activities for all women, single or married, was encouraged, but only as it would help to broaden and increase their capacity as home-makers and mothers. This is the creative physical and spiritual labour which makes woman approach nearest to Godhood."[6]

She had no doubt that great and more marvelous things could take place, and needed to take place, as the kingdom rolled on.

And yes, the tea with Queen Victoria did become a reality. Though tea-drinking had been a part of British culture since 1662, Victoria altered and expanded it to suit her own particular preferences and needs. She would hold what was called Afternoon Tea in the drawing room, and women attending dressed for the event. When the Queen entertained Susan B. Anthony, Susa Gates, and others, she showed sincere, respectful interest in what their views were and what they hoped to accomplish.

Overwhelming as the struggle for women's rights seemed to be, Lucy had seen and lived through the many cruel and heartless, at times nearly unbearable, circumstances which the Saints had been required to overcome, time and time again, clear into the coming of Johnson's Army in the Salt Lake Valley. She had a proven faith in

Heavenly Father's tender support of those who were striving for right and knew also that His timing was not our timing and in this, as in all things, men and women struggling to find their way through mortality must walk by faith.

Susa was in the midst of the fray, but Lucy had options that drew her in other directions. When the Council in London drew to a close, Lucy stayed on, determined to travel to Berlin, Germany, where her granddaughter, Leah Widtsoe, was living with her husband, John. Leah had recently given birth to a baby, a daughter named Anna, and Lucy was anxious to see the child and the young couple and to be of help to them all.

Leah was the daughter of Alma Bailey Dunford, from Susa's first disastrous marriage, and she bore his name. She had also lived with her father and her father's people for most of her growing up years. To have sweet association with her, to see her happily married to a good man, learning and progressing in her own right, was a joy to Lucy, as well as to her mother, Susa.

This time in Berlin was a delightful experience for Lucy: the beautiful forests; the ancient buildings, which included museums and a cathedral which dated to the 1400s; the city, itself, sitting on the banks of the Spree River and first organized and brought to life in the year 1244. Everywhere she looked there was beauty, much of it centered in the Tiergarten, which had been opened nearly 150 years before as a pleasure garden for the citizens. Even the large, imposing streets bore the beauty of their surroundings, culminating in the main avenue of Unter den Linden.

The history of this great culture excited Lucy's senses. She was interested in learning more—and that more included a usable knowledge of the German language, which study she began at once. A quick learner, she soon reached a point where she could communicate well and thus was able to serve—*to be useful.* And that "usefulness" exhibited itself as quickly as it was able. Lucy began by giving talks in church meetings and associating with the women: listening to them, learning of their ways. There were needs here, and one of them was for these women to enjoy the blessings of organization. So Lucy helped to establish the Relief Society and soon was given the responsibility of presiding over the Relief Societies in the German Mission.[7] In

1861 the mission had been closed, and Germany was joined with Switzerland and Italy in one mission. Many of the early converts had immigrated to America, and there had been much persecution of the LDS missionaries from the 1860s on. In 1880 there had been only 280 members in Germany, though in the ensuing years membership grew at increasing numbers, as many as three hundred new converts a year. But not until 1898 was Germany reopened and reestablished as a separate mission again, presided over by Arnold Heinrich Schulthess until 1901.[8] Thus, Lucy's arrival and her willingness to serve were timely.

Actually, at this time both Susa's daughters were in Berlin, so Lucy spent much of her time with Emma Lucy Gates, who was not yet married but grateful for some encouragement and help, as she was struggling valiantly with an extremely demanding and challenging career.

Emma had begun to study music in St. George when she was twelve, concentrating on learning the piano and the violin. It wasn't until she traveled to Goettingen, Germany, intending to continue her study of piano, that her gift for vocal music was awakened in her soul and she knew beyond a doubt what she was meant to do with her talents and her life.

Both of Susa's girls were richly endowed with qualities of spirit, as well as earthly opportunities and earthly gifts. Of Emma Lucy the following praise is representative: "Miss Gates is magnetic, lovely, prudent, a prompt and thorough business woman, exceedingly conscientious and honorable, with a bubbling, vivacious charm which wins friends instantly and forever holds them, as she is unselfishly devoted to them all, and is beloved by all who know her."[9]

Leah held the distinction of being "the first trained Domestic Scientist in the Church and in the West."[10] Her education was impressively extensive, including a degree in pedagogy from BYU in 1898, where she was also the head of the Domestic Science Department. She met John Widtsoe while they were studying at Harvard and married him in the Salt Lake Temple on June 1, 1898. Leah's tenure in

Germany was in support of her husband, that he might earn a degree at the University of Gottingen. All these things, and more, Leah had accomplished before Lucy came to help her after the birth of her daughter—yet another remarkable accomplishment in her young life.

Leah possessed a determined, organized, and far-sighted mind. It was said of her that "as a girl, (she) was strikingly handsome, brilliant and popular."[11] So both girls shared a heritage of brilliance and high purpose, as well as hearts that were tuned to the high standard of loving, giving, and blessing others, which they had learned.

Susa was delighted by the lives her daughters were building for themselves, and she was deeply grateful. Lucy, on her part, knew how fortunate she was to spend this time with her precious granddaughters. She had begun a new decade in her life, and time was becoming a precious commodity, but as always, nothing deterred her. Susa described the conditions in a word picture: "Here she was at age seventy, in a foreign country, living in an apartment 5 floors up, before elevators."[12]

By the summer of 1901, Susa and Jacob were becoming anxious over the long absence of their young daughter, who had been living so far from home for three long years. Lucy returned with Emma, which must have been a comfort to her parents. But the two independent women, cut from much the same cloth, stopped in England before sailing for the United States.

Before her trip to London for the convention, Lucy had already gently dislodged her St. George roots and returned to Salt Lake City, fulfilling a dream of basically designing and building a home as she had envisioned it. It was a beautiful, tasteful home, which pleased Lucy's senses and spoke to her heart.

Susa deeded the property to her mother, and the home, built on what is 705 North 200 West, in the lovely Marmalade Hill area, was completed in 1893. So, Lucy had a place to come home to, and many things to look forward to as well. She had association with both of her daughters there, at least intermittently. Dora had been living in Coeur d'Alene, Idaho, with her husband, Albert Hagan, who had become a well-respected attorney, but he died in 1895. One account says clearly, "Dora lived a full life as a mother and grandmother, later returning to Salt Lake City where she lived until her death of October 21, 1921."[13]

Apparently, Rhoda, who had also been living in Coeur d'Alene for many years, married her third husband, Joseph Sanborn, and they lived in the Salt Lake house likewise until 1903, when they moved to a new house. In 1910, five years following Lucy's death, the little family moved to Seattle, Washington. Rhoda had deeded the house entirely to Lucy, but in 1920 they returned to Salt Lake and, after Lucy was now gone from their midst, Susa and Rhoda regained the property.[14]

Lucy had come full circle. This spot held her beginnings. Here all her growing up into true womanhood came to pass, and she grew as the city grew, as the Saints grew, as the three children God had given her grew. Here it was, eleven years ago, when the grand Salt Lake Temple was dedicated unto the Lord at last, after forty years of faith and dedication, on April 6, 1893. There were four temples in the state of Deseret, and she had been part of them all. She felt grateful the Lord had blessed her so abundantly that she could give an additional sum of $500 to the fund for completing this sacred edifice. That she gave her money anonymously was entirely in keeping with all giving and serving that characterized her life. She was grateful to have been given place in that great gathering room which could contain only a portion of the thousands of Saints thronging the grounds, longing to be inside. Her beginnings and her endings in this Zion to which her beloved Brigham had led them would be in this place.

As this renewed life in the city progressed, Lucy was aware that her health was more fragile, and the pain of rheumatism became more and more of a challenge to her days. Late in 1904 she suffered a fall that was her undoing, forcing her to be consigned to a wheelchair in order to get from place to place. She must have thanked her Father in Heaven many times for the patience she had learned. And she must have sat often in a sunny spot beside a window where she could gaze over the beautiful Valley, retreating into the rich landscape of memory. She knew well how richly she had been blessed, but letting go, realizing that earth life held no further future for her, was the challenge she knew she had to face—and face as well as she had the many others that had entered and altered her years.

A new year arrived: 1905. The Saints, the kingdom, were moving firmly into another century. The year 1805 was when the Prophet Joseph was born. Could one hundred years have passed since that sacred morning, in season with the birth of the Savior, just two days before we celebrate and mark that most sanctified of days? She knew still how uncertain life was. That had not changed, but uncertainty was an element of mortality meant to stretch us, to humble us, to draw us ever closer to the Lord.

For Lucy the hours of the new year would be fleeting. A bad winter cold grew worse and, somehow, she had not the strength with which to fight it. As pneumonia set it, Lucy knew. Her daughters were with her, gentle and united in caring for her. Her spirit hovered, in many ways looking forward now, more than looking back.

February 3 marked Lucy's release from mortality, and her daughters felt the sanctification of the conclusion of a life, of a mortal journey, such as their mother's had been.

Lucy's funeral was held in the 18th Ward chapel on February 6. This was one of the original nineteen wards which Brigham organized when he first began to organize the Valley. Interestingly, he was obviously looking toward the future, for the ward in the beginning consisted of only several families: Brigham Young, Heber C. Kimball, and Newell K. Whitney, and meetings were held in boweries or in Brigham's schoolhouse.[15]

As reported in the *Salt Lake Herald* that day, "This afternoon the funeral services over the remains of Mrs. Lucy Bigelow Young will be held in the Eighteenth ward chapel . . . at 2 o'clock. President Joseph F. Smith will deliver the funeral sermon, Dr. R. B. Pratt who was one of the intimate friends of the family for a great many years will also speak. George D. Pyper's Quartette will furnish music during the services. The internment will take place in the family lot at the city cemetery."[16]

In *The Young Woman's Journal* of 1893 this fitting tribute was written for Lucy: "She has been instrumental in redeeming hundreds of her own dead kindred, while she has ever been joyously willing to take names and assist the poor and unfortunate brethren who need a woman's help in their work in temples.

"No one ever calls upon her for means or for work, for faith or for prayers, in the doing of Christ's work and finds her unwilling or selfish. Of her life she has freely given, and surely she shall in that great eternal work beyond find that precious jewel—eternal lives and glory."[17]

NOTES

1. *SAINTS—No Unhallowed Ground, Volume 2* (Salt Lake City: The Church of Jesus Christ of Latter-day Saints, 2020), 465.
2. Gates, "From Impulsive Girl to Patient Wife: Lucy Bigelow Young," 15.
3. *SAINTS*, 532.
4. "Getting to Know Lucy Bigelow," Brigham Young Granddaughters Association, 13 May 2020, https://www.brighamyounggranddaughters.org/bygablog/2020/3/7/getting-to-know-lucy-bigelow.
5. Ibid.
6. Gates and Widtsoe, *Life Story*, 307–308.
7. Ibid.
8. Schulthesso, "My Ancestor in Church History."
9. Joseph T. Jakeman, ed., *Album Book: Daughters of Utah Pioneersm and Their Mothers* (Salt Lake City: Daughters of Utah Pioneers, 1911), 128.
10. "Mormon Life and Culture", https://www.mormonwiki.com/wiki/index.php?title=leah_Widtsoe_oldid=64030.
11. "Daughters and Their Mothers,"127.
12. "Kari Robinson," Brigham Young Daughters Association, https://www.brighamyoungdaughters.org.
13. Jennifer Ann Mackley, "Find a Grave Memorial," 2014.
14. Jacob Barlow, "Exploring with Jacob Barlow," Thursday, 21 October 2021, JacobBarlow.com, "Rhoda W. Sanborn Home."
15. *The Young Woman's Journal*, volume 4, 300.
16. *Salt Lake Herald*, February 6, 1905.
17. *The Young Woman's Journal*, volume 4, 300.

SUSA YOUNG GATES

CHAPTER SEVEN

SUSA WAS A VIVACIOUS, EXTRAORDINARY PERSON FROM HER VERY beginnings. To her the world was a place of fascination and beauty, a place of possibilities, a place of love. No restrictions were ever placed upon her legitimate goals and aims. Rather, she was surrounded by a myriad of shining examples. In addition to her own father and mother, there were the outstanding "aunts," which was the affection term she used with Brigham Young's other wives. In addition, there were clerks, tradesmen, master craftsmen, gifted singers, seamstresses—the list could go on and on of interesting and capable people who made their own contributions to the richness of her young life.

These were realistic examples, for pioneer life was nothing, if not realistic, demanding, and down to earth. But progress, innovation, cooperation, encouragement, education—these were all elements of Susa's daily existence, living in an atmosphere where she knew she could seize the opportunities offered her, and by application of all her energies and powers, bring the things she desired into realities. There was always assistance when she was in need of it, and she learned to offer assistance to others, which giving, in itself, was part of the enrichment of her inner self.

This, therefore, perhaps subconsciously, and very naturally, became the pattern of her life.

Susa prized her distinction of being the first child born in the Lion House but perhaps grew tired of the humorous story of her birth. Lucy had suffered difficulty in sustaining pregnancy once she had conceived a child. During the confusion prior to Susa's birth, Lucy had but little food to sustain her and was in the habit of sharing even that. She must have been frightened when she lay down on the bed prepared for her and wondered concerning this coming child. Yet, she was surely comforted by the fact that Zina was with her, Zina who had a gift for healing and a gift for loving. Years later, Susa wrote of her, "Sister Zina was all love and sympathy, and drew people after hr by reason of that tenderness."[1] She was powerful spiritually; she had learned the lessons of self-denial and self-forgetfulness, which Lucy was quietly teaching herself.

Another of Brigham's daughters, Clarissa, in writing of life with her father and his family, drew an insightful picture of Zina when she wrote: "It is as the 'Doctor' that she is known best. She had very little training but had a great deal of natural ability which she put to use not only for our own family, but for many others throughout the city. She officiated at the arrival of hundreds of babies. . . . Many of the poor people of the city depended upon her for advice and comfort, as well as for physical ministrations, and she seemed to have a never-ending supply of all three."[2]

Nevertheless, when Zina announced that this child was a second daughter, it may have disappointed Lucy just a little, for her first impulsive response was, "'Shucks!'

"'No,' said Zina, 'it isn't all shucks, it's wheat, and full weight too!'"

Susa was able to make light of the story when she wrote of it or quoted it in public. "'You have a thumbnail sketch of my life ever since. Someone always either inside of me or outside of me, is usually saying 'shucks' after my hurried entrance most anywhere. And I am usually trying to convince my other self and the rest of the folks that 'it's all wheat and full weight at that.' Sometimes I don't care and let it go at 'shucks.'"[3]

The Lion House was a beginning point for many things, including entertainments and recitations by the children. Brigham even had built a platform where the small actors and actresses could perform.

Here, from large hooks secured in the walls, the children could pull taffy or molasses candy. Most of the basement held work rooms of one sort or another, including cellars for dairy goods that needed to be kept cold, cellars for storing apples and vegetables, and a large weaving room that could accommodate both "a great spinning wheel and a weaving loom . . . neither ever idle for any great length of time."[4] The children had part in as many activities and responsibilities as possible and were made to feel at home in every part of their father's vast domain.

Brigham Young believed in fresh air and exercise. He believed in order and careful organization. Reading Susa's account of her childhood is much like reading the descriptions of some idyllic imaginary place that could never really exist. The marvel is in the comprehensive guiding intellect and love that made this life a reality.

For example, the washroom contained two large built-in copper boilers that were heated by a fireplace that sat underneath. The hard work of pounding the clothes with a large wooden hammer was a task allotted to one of the hired men, and each wife had her predetermined day and hour of doing her washing. The drainage and garbage systems were also very effective, so that all elements worked unitedly and well.

The children were fortunate to have Harriet Young as their teacher during these early years. She had experienced a gentle life with her Quaker parents, and her father actually gave her five hundred dollars to assist her in the journey which would take her away from him.

Education was important; therefore, serious business. It was also part of everything in its time and place. The children had a bathhouse in an old wagon, with a roof on top and benches along the side. A clear mountain stream ran through from the canyon, providing a pool. The water was cold much of the year, but that didn't seem to stop any one of them. In all things Brigham had his finger on the pulse of the ideal. He felt it was healthy to sleep out of doors when possible, so the children played on the long porch Brigham had built on the west side of the Lion House, where, Susa writes, "We all took our regular exercises. In the summer this was used as a sleeping porch for the younger members of the family."[5]

Physical recreation enhanced mental acuity. But nothing was more vital, more sacred than learning, which helps us grow closer to the Source of our light. As Susa once expressed it: "The people of this Church have always cherished knowledge and have sacrificed time and means when necessary, for the cause of education. One of the first acts of Brigham Young's administration after the martyrdom of the Prophet in 1844, was to re-open the schools of Nauvoo and to encourage every possible teacher to continue that good work. When driven from Nauvoo and resting beside the Missouri River, schools were taught, under his direction, in Winter Quarters."[6]

The first school in Utah was held in the tent of Mary Dilworth Hammond, in the old Fort, as early as October 1847. Brigham, and some of the other leaders with large families, established schools of their own. Only illness could keep Brigham's children from attending school. In Zina's little adobe house she opened a school, with the children sitting in her living room, until the large room in the Lion House lower floor was provided. Susa's children were certainly taught to value education. It had become, really, a fact of life to them, which helped prepare them for the magnificent work each one accomplished.

Theatre and dance; these two were the best loved of pioneer entertainment, but music was at the heart of it all. "Music," Susa writes in her father's biography, "is the universal language. Its study and practice enlarges the soul and refines the feelings. Music is the only art which is referred to in the Scriptures as a part of heaven itself. It is the reward of the righteous, and the occupation of the angels."[7]

There was an orchestra in Nauvoo, and two bands, one being William Pitt's Nauvoo Brass Band. He and his English friends brought music with them and even imported instruments from their native country. During the struggles of the journey across the plains their music, and that of other bands and choirs, inspired, encouraged, and delighted the weary and heart-sore Saints.

"The word" was held sacred by the early Saints, and poetry was written and admired as much as prose. In fact, it was a unique Scottish convert from Glasgow, Scotland, who worked miracles in missionary work throughout Great Britain and actually published the first entire book of poetry, *Harp of Zion*, within the Church—three years before Eliza R. Snow's first publication i n1856. The two later became friends and compatriots, after he and his family made their way to Zion, and Brother Lyon was much loved and admired by Brother Brigham, other leaders, and most of the LDS artistic community. John Lyon was, interestingly, the chaplain over the whole Jacob Gates Company, which traveled to Zion under direction of Jacob Gates Sr., father of Susa's husband, Jacob Forsberry Gates.

Newspapers and magazines, such as the *Times and Seasons,* and the dramatic arts had their beginning back in Nauvoo, or earlier, under direction and with approval of the Prophet Joseph. Susa reminds the readers of her biography of her father, "When it is remembered that in those days newspapers and American literature generally were just emerging into years of accountability, it is marvelous that so deep an interest was taken in the development of the published word as was manifested by the Latter-day Saints and their leaders."[8]

It mattered not that the Saints had gone to a barren, uninhabited desert. They brought the richness of their society with them, and Susa grew up in the midst of that richness and the happiness it generated.

There had been a dramatic company in Nauvoo, actually formed by the Prophet Joseph. With her usual discernment, Susa says, "The love of wholesome and artistic theatricals was a part of the temperament and policy of Brigham Young."[9] Indeed, he once made this unequivocal statement, variously reported, but saying that if he were ever placed on a desert island and given the task of civilizing a people, the first thing he would do would be to build a theater.

Susa was eager to become adept at telegraphy, which required learning a modified version of the Morse code, accepted as the international standard in 1865. Then there was stenography, which required learning shorthand as well. She had entered the University of Deseret at the age of thirteen, and there, a year later, she became editor of the school magazine. She was her father's daughter with her indefatigable energy and in her curious eagerness to learn, understand, and excel.

Then some subtle but very important changes began to take place. Her sister, Dora, against the strict counsel of her parents, married a sweetheart who was not interested in keeping the standards of the Church. Susa knew this, but she winked at it, so to speak, somehow, in girlish loyalty, supporting her sister and hoping things would turn out all right. They did not seem to be doing so when Susa took another unwise step and married Alma Bailey Dunford, who was the cousin of Dora's husband, Frank Morley Dunford, who went by the name of Morley. Dora had married in 1870; it was now 1872, and Susa was just sixteen years old. She worked hard to convince herself that this marriage would be different. Alma was older. He was an educated dentist, thus having a profession and a maturity that would make a difference. But they did not. He, too, struggled with drink and with other aspects of the gospel.

By this time Lucy Bigelow Young and her two married daughters were living in St. George, and Susa was busy becoming a mother to a son, Bailey, and a daughter, Leah. The sisters spent part of their time back home in Salt Lake, where they both gave birth to a child in August of 1875. Susa was able to return to St. George and work with her father, spending precious time watching and helping as he chiseled out the plans for the St. George Temple. This was a special blessing to Susa as she struggled with the disappointment and guilt of the choice she had made, and the ashes of her hopes, as the sad realities of her life with Alma unfolded. Being a star stenographer, she was allowed the privilege of recording the groundbreaking of the temple, this first temple to be built in the new land to which the Lord had led them.

Five short years and two precious children later, Alma was called on a mission to Great Britain, a practice which was hoped would be helpful to young men who needed to grow up a bit and renew their dedication to the gospel. Susa realized that she was enjoying the peace of her home, without the constant contention to which she had grown accustomed.

Now Susa was divorcing Alma, "when she could no longer live with his drinking and abuse. One night, after he had been drinking, he had thrown Susie and their six-month-old daughter, Leah, out of the house, yelling at them to never come back."[10] But as the horrors of her decision unfolded, she could hardly bear them. At first she lost legal custody of both her children, though custody of Bailey was given her, but Leah was entirely lost to her for many years.

This was in the year 1877, the year Brigham Young died. But before his death, Susa brought another matter to his attention, one that was close to her heart. Under Brigham's direction, the Relief Societies had been reorganized in 1867, and the prophet had also "instigated multiple Schools of the Prophets . . . from 1867 through 1874, with over nine hundred members eventually meeting in Salt Lake City and an additional five thousand members in branch schools formed in other towns."[11]

The Saints had always been a people apart, maintaining their identity as "an holy nation" and, through unity, service and faith, growing closer to the ideal of children of God, functioning, serving, learning under His direction. Cohesiveness was being re-established and, as part of this, some of the leading Sisters of the Relief Society had collaborated with Professor Tullidge to produce a book entitled *Women of Mormondom*. The women who came up with the three dollars to purchase and read it were excited and pleased with what they saw.

Susa was twenty-one years old, just on the brink of growing up, despite the things which she had experienced and suffered. Eliza R. Snow wrote her a letter wherein she stated, "We are thinking of sending a few staunch sisters to the States to canvass for the sale of it."[12] She was inviting Susa, who had worked on the book, to go! A national speaking tour, with both Aunt Eliza and Aunt Zina, would be like a foretaste of heaven and perfect preparation for all the writing and achieving Susa intended to do as her opportunities expanded.

This was her father's last chance. Perhaps he knew, or at least sensed that. He knew his daughter well. He knew of her ambitions, her desires, her gifts. At this crucial point, with all the wisdom he possessed, with all the love he held for her, he warned her gently, but with that surety and firmness that was his nature, against seeking the success and acclaim of the world, on setting her heart upon things that would subtly draw her away from all that really mattered.

"'If you were to become the greatest woman in the world,' he told her, 'and you should neglect your duty as wife and mother, you would wake up on the morning of the First Resurrection and find you had failed in everything.'" His counsel left no gray areas, but he did add, "'All that you can do after you have satisfied the righteous claims of your home and family, will redound to your credit and to the honor and glory of God.'"[13]

Her father's counsel took root deep in Susa's heart and became the guiding impulse to all she chose, to every path she followed, from that day on.

Brigham had said the same thing of himself, applying the same powerful eternal principle, truly understanding that if he succeeded in all things and failed as a husband and father, he would have failed indeed.

Susa listened. She could not keep her spirit from responding to the spirit of her father, and she was further molded in the direction which would bring her true greatness to the fore, as a blessing to herself and to others.

NOTES

1. "Zina D. H. Young, Third President of the Relief Society , 1888–1901," https://www.churchofjesuschrist.org/callings/relief-society/relief-society-presidents/zina-h-young?lang=eng.
2. Spencer and Harmer, *Brigham Young at Home*, 77.
3. Burgess-Olsen, *Sister Saints*, 64.
4. Spencer and Harmer, *Brigham Young at Home*, 28.
5. Gates and Widtsoe, *Life Story*, 325.
6. Ibid., 283.
7. Ibid., 239.
8. Ibid., 370.
9. Ibid., 272.
10. *SAINTS*, chapter 43, "A Greater Necessity for Union," with Emily Utt, curator, Utah Historic Sites Division of Church History Department, podtail.com/podcast/saints-podcast/43-9-greater-necessity-for-union/, 6.
11. Madsen Derr and Grow Holbrook, *First Fifty Years of Relief Society, Part 3.* 1867–1879, 2.
12. Ibid., 1.
13. SAINTS, volume 2, 440.

Chapter Eight

———— ∾⊕⌇ ————

She must learn. She must progress. She must not dwell upon those things that would drag her down with remorse and sorrow. The solution that spoke to Susa's mind was the Brigham Young Academy. Karl G. Maeser, whom she had known and learned from as a child, had been appointed principal just the year before and was to serve in this capacity for sixteen years. To Maeser a person's morals and character were of greater importance than his intellect. He applied the counsel Brigham had given him: to teach nothing, not even the multiplication tables, without the Spirit of the Lord. Thus, under his tutelage, the school became a unique and exceptional place.

Susa was gifted in music; all of Brigham's children possessed musical talents to some extent. She could see that there was work to be done, so she convinced Maeser to allow her to organize and establish a music department. She was happy in the work. She wrote in detail to her mother: "Really mother dear you can scarcely realize the amount of work I have done lately. The Academy Choir (under me of course) learned ten, choruses, and anthems, in two weeks. I am obliged to sing each part with everyone as I did in the old club. It is indeed *very* wearing on the lungs and nerves. But I love it, and am so glad I can assist the fresh young, and often times sweet singers of Zion to praise God in melody and in song.

"During the Conference here we sang for the Twelve who were here, and Bros. [John] Taylor, [Daniel H.] Wells, [Brigham] Young [Jr.], and [George F.] Gibbs expressed themselves highly pleased with our music. Both Bro. Taylor and Sister E[liza] R. Snow expressed the very kindest feelings for me, and seemed to feel a great interest in my course."[1]

Nevertheless, Susa was frustrated and restless. Her daughter was living far from her in Bear Lake, and what was happening there? Susa felt the agony of self-blame and self-doubt. Could she really ever alter her life and the lives of her children, and be happy again?

Susa jumped at the opportunity which came for her to visit the Sandwich Islands, for she knew her dear friend, Jacob Gates, from her St. George days, was on a mission there. She and Zina, her father's widow to whom she was so close, traveled together, going by carriage from Honolulu after they arrived, to Laie, where the greater number of Latter-day Saints was gathered. It was a hazardous mountain journey, but both women were eager to reach their destination and were pleased to be greeted with a celebration of a meal, dancing, and song. On the islands, "roughly one in every twelve Hawaiians was a Latter-day Saint."[2]

Their proposed stay was to last two months. It was time to learn the ways of the people a little, to help reorganize Relief Society, to love and encourage, and Zina planned a commemoration of the second anniversary of Brigham Young's death. The older woman, in tenderness, realized from the start that Susa would be spending a good portion of her time in courting.

In her heart Susa knew. There was such a sweet confidence in her relationship with this goodly man. They were able to take little trips up into the canyon together. In a careful love letter to him Susa wrote, "I am thinking of you now, away up in the hills. Are you wishing, like me, that work had not to be done today, that we might talk over the future and express in a thousand ways that in our minds?"[3]

She left for home with mixed feelings. In tenderness, she wrote to Jacob, "God is good, and He will help me to pick up the shattered threads of life and mend them into something useful."[4]

She had learned well from Lucy's loving example, which had been always before her. Susa knew she had work to do for the kingdom and, despite her failings, she knew the Lord would help her to be useful, if she would just go forward with faith in Him.

On January 5, 1880, Susa and Jacob married. In that same year the Church celebrated its fiftieth year with a jubilee which included a major reorganization of the women. Louisa Felt was nominated to stand at the head of all the Primaries of the Church, and Elmira Taylor as general president of the Girl's Mutual Improvement Association (MIA)—both of these sisters having counselors selected and appointed as well. It seemed only natural that Eliza R. Snow become president of the women's Relief Society, choosing Elizabeth Ann Whitney and Zina Young as her counselors. A First Presidency was also selected to stand at the head of the Church as when Brigham had been alive. John Taylor was sustained as president with George Q. Cannon and Joseph F. Smith as his counselors. Another important step took place. At George Q. Cannon's motion, the Church membership moved to accept the Pearl of Great Price as an official part of the scripture canon of the Church, what were called the standard works. There was great unity among the Saints, and a sense of oneness and progress. Much had happened, many trials and hardships had been met and overcome, and marvelous things had occurred since their gathering in Utah. What might the next fifty years bring?

This progressiveness was part of Susa's life as well. It felt good to have a life of happiness, good works, and well-being. But, all of a sudden, in the autumn of 1885, President Taylor asked Jacob to serve a second mission to Hawaii. Everything had changed in his life in the ensuing six years: he had married Susa and they were living in Provo. They had three children together who they were beginning to raise, and Susa was expecting another. And little Bailey still lived with his mother and her new husband, part of this growing family.

How could they make such a change? The prophet had given Jacob but three brief weeks to prepare! This seemed almost an impossibility. And what of his family—might he be allowed to take them with him? When Jacob asked the question outright, he received no reply, so Susa's preparations, for the time being, were for her husband alone. She struggled against discouragement when she learned that three other missionaries had already received such permission, and living space on the island Susa knew was sorely limited. Then incredulity produced a new set of fears when, just a week before the scheduled departure, permission was unexpectedly granted!

With that decision, a period of great challenges and trials ensued. Susa quickly wrote to her ex-husband, Alma Dunford, asking his permission to let her take Bailey with her. The boy was ten years old; surely his father would consider this as all right. But Alma knew that he still held power of the court over Susa and waited, cruelly, until she and Jacob were actually gathered with their family at the train station in Salt Lake to march up and, with a court order and a deputy, forbid her taking her son.

Susa had no power; she had no recourse. She was forced to watch her little boy dissolve into tears and beg to be allowed to remain with his mother. What bitter, bitter fruits! She must turn her back and somehow go on!

Susa was ill on the voyage, which was nothing but a misery to her. She tried her best to rally when a large group of Saints met them upon their arrival and when Joseph F. Smith came forth to gently greet her. She had nearly forgotten that he was exiled on the island. This was the first note of hope that had come. Joseph F. and Julina were dear friends. They would succor and aid her, and she would somehow find the strength and spirit with which to go on.

It took Susa a while to adjust, and she grew tired easily, a bit overwhelmed by her pregnancy, and the extent of her domestic duties of cooking, laundry, and sewing new clothing, more appropriate to the climate, for her children. She had a six-year-old, a four-year-old, a three-year-old, and an infant. And the ways here were different from anything she knew. At the same time she was trying to write and send articles off to newspapers. She must not be forgotten. She must not lose her place in that world. She tried hard not to think about it and to just carry on.

She was so distracted that when four-year-old Jay developed a cough, and then a fever, she let herself suppose that it was only a cold. But a week passed, and the symptoms did not go away but grew worse. It relieved Susa's heart when Joseph F. Smith came to bless her little suffering son. She was encouraged by the faith she felt. But the illness did not lessen nor go away.

It was the night of February 22. Would Susa ever forget? She stayed up with her son, rubbing his little tummy with oil and murmuring a mother's encouragement. He begged her not to leave him, and she promised she would not. But then he seemed to fall into an easy sleep, and Jacob urged her to get some much-needed rest. Wisely or unwisely, he did not tell her that their little boy had awakened in the night, calling and calling for her. In the morning when Susa gazed at her son, did she sense that the look of death was upon him?

Joseph F. and Julina came and stayed close beside them. What could anyone do? In the afternoon, just before two, Jay began to rest peacefully and died in his sleep.

Horrified, Joseph and Julina remained with their dear friends. They had lost their daughter, Josephine, when she was very near this age. They could understand, they could agonize with Jacob and Susa, but they could not change the pain, nor alter the overriding sense of guilt and failure that rested on the young mother's heart.

Susa was too stunned, too overwhelmed to know what to do, to know how to mourn. The Saints fasted and prayed for them, but they and their remaining children were placed under quarantine, for little three-year-old Karl came down with the same dreaded diphtheria and quickly grew worse. Soon after, he was taken by death from them, too. They felt removed from any sense of aid or reality.

Susa was unable to grieve along with her husband. She was too worried about her children who yet lived and breathed in this fragile state of survival. And she was worried about the child she was carrying; waiting, listening, finding herself holding her breath. Was this child still alive within her? She could not really share her fears with anyone else. But when at last she felt a definite flutter of life, she wrote of the experience and sensations to the one with whom she had shared everything from the beginning—her mother.

"A very faint motion comforts me with hope that life still beats under my saddened heart.'" She was not allowing her thoughts to go too far, in an agonized attempt to understand what purposes might lay behind the deaths of her sons. "'With all this,'" she continued to

Lucy, "'we know that God rules in the heavens. God has blessed me and helped me to bear my burdens. Praise his holy name forever.'"[5]

Susa's response here recorded is incredibly insightful and spiritually humbling to any who read and ponder her words. She was human, and she did desire to achieve and excel at the thing she did well, with the gifts she had been given. But her heart was always here, in this place. It had been trained early, and it did not falter. In one of her letters to her mother from BYA, in April 1879, she confided: "I care nothing for the fame of the world, but here my few small talents are being daily improved, my sphere of usefulness is being enlarged, and how much happier am I than as though forced to go through a daily routine of work distasteful to me. . . . Yes, dearest mother, I am trying to forget all that was, all that might have been, and make myself contented and happy here. I humbly thank God for all his blessings, and want to be worthy of His goodness to me."[6]

The days of missionary work in the islands continued. Grief sat like a shadow on Susa's heart, and she found herself watching her children with a tense concentration, looking for any signs of impending illness.

Finding time to write, energy to write, the quiet necessary to create, was perhaps her biggest challenge. Her mornings began early, and her daily tasks seemed endless. But her desire to write for the *Exponent* magazine continued to grow.

In 1888 the Gates's mission was drawing to a close. Taking the matter in hand, encouraged by Jacob's interest and support, Susa wrote to Zina Young, confessing her desires and outlining some of her ideas for the future of the *Exponent*. "My whole soul is for the building up of this kingdom," she declared. "I would labor so hard to help my sisters. The work would be a labor of love, for you know I love writing."[7]

The *Woman's Exponent* was one of the first magazines for women in the world. It was founded under the direction of Eliza R. Snow and the encouragement of Brigham Young. Lulu Green (Richards), a niece of the prophet's, became the first editor. Susa said of it: "From this time onward the *Exponent* is the unfolding celluloid upon which is screened the pulsating woman's life of that rapidly developing period—not only in Zion, but all over the world. Its founders and editors received constant and material help and encouragement from the leaders. Its usefulness to the women of the Church may scarcely be overestimated."[8]

But this was not destined to be the course for Susa's usefulness to take!

Nothing in her life was of greater importance to Emmeline B. Wells than her work at the *Exponent* and the control she was able to exercise there. Not until 1877 did she become the editor, but she held the coveted position for thirty-seven years. The course of her life in the kingdom had been a rocky one. Following a somewhat privileged childhood, she had married a childhood sweetheart, James Harris, son of the branch president in New Salem, Massachusetts. He was only sixteen—and she a year younger. They were two children going off on a grand adventure together.

Emmeline never forgot the overwhelming power of her first impression when she looked upon the Prophet Joseph's face in the spring of 1844. But the wondrous world opening up before them was cut cruelly short with the murder of Joseph and Hyrum Smith in Carthage on June 27, and the horror, confusion, and apostasy that followed. James's parents left the Church. Emmeline gave birth to her first child—a beautiful little boy who was to be her only son, and who died six short weeks later. James, frightened and distraught, went up the Mississippi River in search of work—and never returned. She met the boats as they came, and watched and waited. "In her diary of February 20, 1845, nine days before her seventeenth birthday, she wrote: 'When will sorrow leave my bosom! All my days have I experienced it, oppression has been my lot. . . . Here am I brought to this great city . . . and left dependent on the mercy and friendship of strangers. . . . Must I forever be unhappy, wilt the time never come when happiness and enjoyment will be the lot of this lump of clay?'"[9]

Her hopes rose when she was accepted as a plural wife by Newell and Elizabeth Ann Whitney, traveling across the plains with them, looking upon her new husband more as a father than anything and loving his good, gentle wife. She bore two daughters, the second shortly after arriving in the Valley in October 1848. "But six weeks later, the gentle Newel Whitney died suddenly, leaving a bereaved and stunned family. Emmeline was a widow twice by the time she was twenty-two."[10]

She and her children had to live. At last, exhausted and discouraged—and, truth being stranger than fiction—Emmeline penned a letter to one of Newel's best friends, Daniel H. Wells, who was already a polygamist, "asking him to 'consider the lonely state of his friend's widow' and accept her as a wife."[11]

As Emmeline wrote in response to Susa, "My dear young and gifted friend, I do not feel that you will be in your best situation as a member or partner in the *Exponent*." Romania Pratt was another dear friend who had become the first woman doctor in Utah and also contributed to the *Exponent*. She suggested that Susa think of starting a new magazine—one that could serve the youth of the Church.[12]

Who better to advise Susa than her dear and trusted friend, Joseph F. Smith, who was all encouragement and support? She did not stop there but wrote to the Young Ladies presidency and to President Woodruff as well. She met with only approval and confidence.

Perhaps she was remembering things that were deeply ingrained in her mind. It was her father who began the movement for Young Women, starting with his own household, his own daughters. In her *Life Story of Brigham Young* Susa describes it in vivid detail. Speaking in the parlor of the Lion House on November 28, 1869, Brigham, as was his customary habit, minced no words:

> All Israel is looking to my family and watching the example set by my wives and children. For this reason, I desire to organize my own family first into a society for the promotion of habits of order, thrift, industry, and charity; and above all things, I desire them to retrench from their extravagance in dress, in eating and even in speech. The time has come when the sisters must agree to give up their follies of dress and cultivate a modest apparel, a meek deportment, and to set an example worthy of imitation before the people of the world. . . . I want you to set your own fashions. Let your apparel be neat and comely, and the workmanship of your own hands. . . . There is need for the young daughters of Israel to get a living testimony

of the truth. I wish our girls to obtain a knowledge of the Gospel for themselves. For this purpose I desire to establish this organization and want my family to lead out in the great work. . . . Retrench in everything that is not good and beautiful. Not to make yourselves unhappy, but to live so that you may be truly happy in this life and the life to come.[13]

The prospects looked promising, but Susa was wise enough to write in her journal, "Well, it is in the hands of the Lord."[14]

NOTES

1. Godfrey, Godfrey, Derr. *Women's Voices*, 335–36.
2. *SAINTS*, volume 2, 471.
3. Susa Young Gates Papers/Susa Young to Jacob Gates, Aug. 13, 1879, Chapter 6.
4. Gates Papers. Susa Young Gates to Jacob Gates, Feb. 3, 1879, Chapter 1.
5. Jacob F. Gates Papers/Susa Young Gates Papers. Susa Young Gates to Lucy Bigelow Young. March 6, 1887, Chapter 1.
6. Godfrey, Godfrey, Derr. *Women's Voices*, 334.
7. *SAINTS*, volume 2, 559–560.
8. Susa Young Gates to Zina Huntindon Young, 5 May 1888, "Susa Young Gates," https://www.churchofjesuschrist.org/study/history/topics/susa-young-gates
9. Susan Evans McCloud, *Women of the Restoration* (Springville, Utah: CFI, 2020), 90. Quoted in Madsen, *In Their Own Words*, 45.
10. Ibid., 91. Quoted in *Wells: Defender: The Life of Daniel H. Wells*.
11. *SAINTS*, volume 2, 560.
12. Gates and Widtsoe, *Life Story*, 305–306.
13. Ibid., 201.
14. *SAINTS*, volume 2, 561.

CHAPTER NINE

Now Susa truly began to establish herself as a writer. The *Young Woman's Journal* came to life in 1889 as a monthly magazine. Susa was the spirit behind every page and did much of the writing and editing herself, as well as continuing to contribute to other magazines and newspapers, a habit she kept up for the rest of her life. In 1885 Susa had already written a lovely account entitled *Lydia Knight's History,* and this was to be just the first of published volumes of her own. Later, as her published works increased, Susa even wrote an account of her sufferings in the islands into a small book entitled *The Little Missionary.*

In 1886–87 the Relief Society was re-established among the women of the Church. A week before, President Brigham Young had organized the brethren into several Schools of the Prophets, because membership had quickly risen to over nine hundred in Salt Lake alone, and to more than five thousand in the many branch schools in other towns.

Increased organization appealed to Susa, and though she was challenged by the duties of raising a family and establishing a new literary journal, she began to involve herself wherever she felt she could be useful. This same year of 1889 she was appointed as a member of the Young Ladies Mutual Improvement Board, serving there for more than twenty years. She also helped develop a printed guide for the girls with lessons, instructions, and ideas for beautifying oneself within and without one's environment. One of the favorite saying was, "One cheerful face in a household will keep everything bright—put envy, selfishness, despondency to shame and flight."[1] Susa challenged the girls with the power and beauty of idealism in their efforts to wean themselves away from worldly paths. Tuesday night became "Mutual night" through the valleys, and was respected and taken into account as late as the 1950s and 60s.

The girls of the Church responded with love and enthusiasm to the love Susa brought to everything she wrote and spoke and gave to them. She became known among them, affectionately, as "Aunt Susa."

Two years later, in 1891, Susa founded the Utah Women's Press Club, served on the Board of Trustees for Brigham Young University, and organized the domestic science department there. She also served on the board of the Utah State Agricultural College, organized the Utah Chapter of Daughters of the American Revolution and the state chapter of the Utah Pioneers, became National Chairman of the Press Committee of the US National Women's Council, and in 1902 became the only US delegate to the International Women's Congress in Copenhagen. The list goes on and on from here. Susa knew her voice could be raised for good and her efforts make a difference. She could not refrain from doing all she could to help and bless others, to open doors for women to be educated, and to enjoy opportunities that would help them to advance. Susa was also happily recognized by her friends as a gracious hostess and excellent cook. One might wonder what daily life must have been like for such a woman as this. "In her 'Notes for the Day's Work' we gain powerful insight.

Notes for the Day's Work: Provo, Utah, August 19, 1895

Go down cellar with Emma Lucy [later a world-famous coloratura soprano] and show her how to clean it.

Go to Aunt Corneel's and take her to Eikens and get hers and my fruit. Darn Dan's stockings. Boil over the bottle of spoiled fruit.

Practice on my bicycle. Write down plan of altering the house which came to me in the night.

Clean my office. Answer Leah's, Sterling's, Sis. Taylor's, and Mrs. Grey's letters, and Carlos's. Prepare talk on 'Women and Literature' and go to the [Brigham Young] Academy's opening exercises at 10 o'clock.

Talk to Aretta Young about her story. Write to Pres. Joseph F. Smith, Pres. George Q. Cannon, Apostle Franklin D. Richards, and Elder B. H. Roberts about writing for *Young Woman's Journal.* Also write Mrs. M. E. Potter and Marie D.

Write and thank Carol for her lovely gift. Get the cloth for Dan's pants and boys' clothes and send them to the tailor. Finish the last chapter of "John Stevens' Courtship" for *The Contributor.* Sketch out editorials for *Young Woman's Journal.*

Wash my head. Get the kitchen carpet and have the girl and Dan put it down. Get cot and crib from store. Also washstand and glass and wardrobe. Get vegetables and fruit for dinner. Take my bicycle dress over to Polly and have it fixed. Take clothes to the Relief Society. Get consecrated oil. Bless Cecil [B. Cecil Gates, later director of the Mormon Tabernacle Choir] to do his chores well. Administer to baby Franklin [later an outstanding figure in early days of radio][2]

A bit daunting to the reader. Perhaps Susa moved quickly, worked quickly—and wrote quickly!

The early days of the *Young Woman's Journal* were challenging. The Church had no money to give them, so Susa had to finance the printing by subscriptions at $2.00 yearly. But the magazine was still in debt to the *Juvenile Instructor* press. So she girded up her loins and canvassed the state, urging the Saints to support and subscribe. Through her efforts and faith Susa was able to increase subscriptions so markedly that the price could be cut in half! By 1910 the number had reached between 14 and 15,000 subscribers, and the magazine continued successful until October 1929, nearly twenty years longer when it was combined with the Young Men's MIA *Improvement Era.*

The *Young Woman's Journal* was warm and personal in tone, and versatile in subject matter, offering opportunities for girls and women both to submit poetry, travel articles, home management articles, articles on taste in clothing, and opinions on how to raise children. Women submitted nostalgic essays about life in the early Church, and many testimonies of the Prophet Joseph and the Gospel were also submitted. Susa's advice and encouragement to the girls' was open and diverse.

There was always a large literary department where stories, essays, and poetry were printed. Other offerings included, "Floral Department," "Temple Workers" "Etiquette," "Health and Hygiene,"

"Historical Sketches," "History of Joseph Smith," "How I Gained My Testimony of the Truth," "Correspondence," "Theological Department," and "Miscellaneous" to cover a variety of things which did not quite fit in elsewhere.

A charming example under the heading of "Etiquette of Picnics" in the August 1894 Issue is characteristic:

> Send out your invitations to a picnic at least two weeks in advance. Let them be verbal or written. The latter is the better plan. Select a convenient and attractive place . . . near a spring or a running stream . . . the ladies usually provide the food and the gentlemen the fruit and drinks. Provide for an extra number of guests, as you may add to your list at the last moment . . . it is better and merrier that all should meet at some designated place . . . and proceed in a body to the place chosen . . . Every gentleman should carry an umbrella, and every lady should take her gossamer and some light wrap.[3]

From the beginning, Susa emphasized the magazine "as an outlet for the literary gifts of the girl members . . . while representing the truths of the Gospel of Jesus Christ."[4] Her spirit, Susa's spirit, moved through all the pages of the *Journal*. She contributed in a dozen different ways, and all she wrote was honest, informative yet tender, and always had an underlying current of the spiritual ideal.

She sometimes wrote under different names, Homespun being her favorite. In Volume IV, Number 12, September 1893, in the "Editorial Department," Susa wrote with great feeling and candor under title of "Not My Will." She explored her progress from a child-like asking to learning to pray and fast, to wait and listen, to realize that blessing always come after she would do this, but often not the ones for which she was praying! She learned "that I must not seek to bind the will of God to suit my own desires. Lately, there has come to me a most beautiful feeling, that of infinite trust and reliance upon every event that transpires in my life. It is all right; everything is all right.

"If only I, this cumbersome, heavy, willful, disobedient I, can keep the laws of God, what is anything that happens to me? Nothing but a providence of God, and therefore to be received joyfully."[5]

Susa had suffered all the things she implies here, and more. Thus, her testimony was one of great power and truth. She told of almost miraculous experiences she had been given and then urged the girls with these words:

"Dearest sisters, if we can only put ourselves unreservedly in the hands of our Heavenly Father, we are sure to learn so much more rapidly and happily all the lessons we have come here to learn. And it is such supreme happiness to know, not to think or suppose, but to know that God will order all things for our best good . . . all and more than I prayed for came, only in the Lord's time, not mine."[6]

Susa exerted an illimitable effect upon the young people of the Church. Spencer W. Kimball, a prophet from somewhat later times, preserved and shared one such choice occurrence:

"My greatest adventure, however, was the reading of the Holy Bible. From infancy I had enjoyed the simplified and illustrated Bible stories, but the original Bible seemed so interminable in length, so difficult to understand, that I avoided it until a challenge came to me from Sister Susa Young Gates. She was the speaker at the MIA meeting of stake conference and gave a discourse on the value of reading the Bible. In conclusion she asked for a showing of all who had read it through. The hands that were raised out of that large congregation were so few and so timid! . . . I was shocked into an unalterable determination to read that great book. As soon as I reached home after the meeting I began with the first verse of Genesis and continued faithfully every day. . . approximately a year later I reached the last verse in Revelation: 'He which testifieth these things saith, Surely I come quickly. Amen. Even so, come, Lord Jesus. The grace of our Lord Jesus Christ be with you all. Amen.'

"What a joy it was to me . . . for more than half a century now I have continued to be grateful to Sister Gates for the inspiration that provoked me to read the Holy Bible my first time."[7]

There was a great deal of tension in the Church as the year 1893 drew to a close. Political issues, especially regarding polygamy and the recent Manifesto, ran high. Many did not know what to do or what to think, and felt a great uncertainty concerning the years ahead.

At the same time, there was a great spiritual push to finish the Salt Lake Temple and dedicate it to the Lord at last. Money was required, and extra working hours among the brethren and sisters if all aspects of the great temple were to be completed. There was still so much actual work to be done, and so many hands were needed. Forty years was a long time. Many who had seen the temple begun were no longer here. The reality of worshipping and performing ordinances in this place seemed almost an impossibility to many minds.

A date was selected just twelve days before the scheduled dedication for a Church-wide fast. The prophet and other leaders felt that the Saints needed humility and a spiritual reconciliation with their Father in Heaven if His spirit was to bless and sanctify this most sacred occasion with harmony and with power from on high. There had been much disunion and spiritual and political turmoil among the people in the early 1890s. The Edmunds Tucker Act had followed the Church Manifesto in 1890, and there was a dismantling of the "people's party"—which was a distinctive part of the belief structure of many of the Latter-day Saint people. This opened a way for accepting the Democratic and Republican parties, and struggles ensued in striving to discern issues and determine what changes and what candidates presaged good and which did not. There was more contention among the Saints than they had ever seen in the Valleys of the Mountains.

As Brother Olmstead explained: "Such contentions caused concerns about whether the Saints were worthy to dedicate a temple—one meant to fulfill the prophecy of Isaiah—and whether the Lord would accept their offering because of their sins against one another. As a response to these worries, a Church-wide fast was held prior to the dedication as the Saints sought forgiveness and apologized for the wrongs they had done to each other. As a result, themes of unity and forgiveness were a central focus in the dedicatory prayers of the temple beginning on April 6, marking the Lord's acceptance of their sacrifices."[8]

Upon this very day Susa received a letter from her daughter, Leah. She was now nineteen, a young woman in her own right, attending college in Salt Lake City. Susa trembled with a variety of emotions when she read that Leah desired reconciliation with her mother. This also surprised her a little, for the two had just argued earlier that week concerning the old issue of Leah's father and Susa's ex-husband. She had trouble accepting her daughter's assessment of the man and of her life with him, even though he had remarried and raised his children, Leah included, in the Church. There was so much more behind it all in Susa's eyes. And the realization that her precious daughter's childhood had been snatched from her had been nearly more than she could bear throughout the years. What father, even the best of fathers, could ever replace the unique love and intimacy between a woman and her daughter?

The matter was so delicate. Leah had apologized, writing, "I humbly and truly repent and beg that you will forgive and forget."[9]

Susa did not want Leah to struggle with guilt and remorse. But she realized that this was exactly what she was doing. It was impossible for Susa to forget, to ever lose the impress of her father's words to her, that if she should succeed at all things and fail as a mother, she would have failed indeed. She knew the adversary desired the misery of both herself and her daughter, and that frightened her, too. She remembered the hope in her heart four years before, when Leah was only fifteen, and they had met at the Lion House—where everything had begun, even Susa's life itself. In this place they wept together, and the unity they felt was as warm, as natural as if they had been sisters, not mother and daughter.

What of the here and now? Susa prayed mightily, with her spirit as open to the promptings of the Lord as she could make it. She attended the fast meeting in Provo and was able to go home and write: "My dearest, darling girl, know that I love you better every day. I know I am far from perfect. Perhaps the greatest sting of your words was, for me, in the fact that in a measure I deserved it. . . . By prayer and a little effort on our part, we can learn to let these things alone. Give me a kiss and bury it forever."[10]

The mighty temple, forty years in the building, the adorning, the praying and the sacrifice, was at last ready to be presented into the hands of the Lord. Just a year earlier, on April 6, 1892, the ceremony of laying the capstone of the great temple had been observed by many thousands of Saints, with prayer and thanksgiving.

There were to be thirty-one sessions to the dedication, beginning on April 6 through April 24, with two dedicatory sessions a day. Hundreds of men had worked, in one way or another, on this sacred edifice. Hundreds of families had sacrificed. The work and faith and sacrifice of many, many Saints would be acknowledged only by the divine hand which had placed them here. The countless prayers and offerings sent up into the ears of the Lord would be seeing fulfillment this day.

Some remained who remembered the beginnings. Lucy was in this first vast congregation with Jacob Gates. Her beloved Susa was sitting at a special recorder's table in the east end of the vast room, where she would have the honor of recording, in the shorthand she had learned so well, this dedication that, in some ways, could not help but transcend all others.

Lucy was one who remembered. She was not there when Brigham Young walked on July 28, four days following his arrival in the Valley, to the spot of earth on that vast expanse, struck his cane into the ground, and stated, "Here we will build a temple to our God." But she, and how many others, recalled the prayers that accompanied the Brethren's efforts to cover up the foundation of the temple when Johnston's Army was threatening to come through, and she was one of the thousands who took what little they could manage and, in faith and patience, crossed the wide Point of the Mountain to Utah Valley, where the little settlement of Provo happily took them in.

Susa, fulfilling this holy calling, was laden with many thoughts and memories, and felt cleansed by gratitude which, like a light, permeated all other emotions of her heart.

NOTES

1. "Young Women," *Encyclopedia of Mormonism*, 1.
2. Susan Evans McCloud, "Heroines of the Restoration", 236–37, from Leonard J. Arrington, "Women As a Force In the History of Utah," *Utah Historical Quarterly 38* (Winter 1970): 5-6.
3. Gates, Susa Young, "Etiquette of Picnics," *Young Woman's Journal*, volume V, August 1894, 552.
4. Gates, *Young Woman's Journal*, volume 40, October 1919, 678.
5. Gates, *Young Woman's Journal*, volume 4, September 1893, 570.
6. Ibid., 571–72.
7. Spencer W. Kimball, "Reading, a Sacred Privilege," *Friend*, November 1978, https://www.churchofjesuschrist.org/study/liahona/1979/09/reading-a-sacred-privilege?lang=eng.
8. "A Greater Necessity For Union," *SAINTS: No Unhallowed Hand*, 659, https://www.churchofjesuschrist.org/study/history/saints/-2?lang=eng
9. Ibid. Leah Dunford's apology to her mother, 659.
10. Ibid. Susa Young Gates in letter to daughter, Leah Dunford, 660.

Chapter Ten

Susa relied on the foundation which was established from her earliest childhood: the gospel, supported by the Church, both supported by the family. In the deepest part of her soul, everything she did, she did for the kingdom. Her involvement in important movements and new and vital organizations was colossal. Her personality was pragmatic, dealing with issues and challenges in sensible, practical, realistic ways. She also, despite trials and even issues of health, possessed the energy to match her commitments, and the heart, or vision, to carry them out as she desired.

An example of the methods by which she lived was revealed in an IOU from her husband, Jacob, which stated his promise "to pay Susa Young Gates Two Hundred Dollars with interest at one per cent per month from date without defalcation or discount. She saw no reason not to use available resources to help loved ones:

"He that will not help his own from some mistaken sentiment is, after all, a poor father. We are willing to give our children money, property, schooling, etc. etc. but we all make a fuss if we or any of our friends help children out in getting established in life. This, I cannot understand and never have."[1]

Women's suffrage was one of the main issues which leading Latter-day Saint women supported. It was a fascinating situation, nearly unbelievable, that gave Mormon women the vote as early as 1870—not through any genuine concern for their welfare but in many ways supported in the East by those who despised the Mormons and polygamy, and falsely believed that if the women in Utah had the vote, they would legislate polygamy out of existence.

With the ironic realities of the time, the privilege was snatched out of their hands by the passage of the Edmunds-Tucker Act against polygamists in 1887, and following that, it was a great struggle to join forces in fighting for their rights all over again.

Susa was in Hawaii fighting her own battles in 1887, and her son, Cecil Brigham, was born that year. It was after this that she attended the International Convention of Women in London, which was the same year that the mission to the Sandwich Islands came to a close.

This was also the year Susa was appointed to the Young Ladies Mutual Improvement Association General Board. And, with this involvement, Susa brought another of her dreams into reality.

Susa had long desired what she described as "an outlet for the literary gifts of the girl members . . . while representing the truths of the Gospel of Jesus Christ."

·Two years later she founded the Utah Women's Press Club, and the following year, in 1892, she was appointed to the Brigham Young University Board of Trustees.

To be in the forefront did not denote prominence to Susa. It indicated dedication and much, much hard work. For instance, the Daughters of Utah Pioneers faced many struggles in getting their organization off the ground. For some time they held meetings in houses of their various members, but it was difficult for board meetings to be held in these circumstances. When Susa was made president in 1905, after difficulties in using the Deseret News building, she arranged for "the use of several commodious rooms in the Lion House." And Susa, facing the realities, reminded the women, "The treasury must depend upon entertainments and entrance fees for its support, and the semi-yearly entertainments of the society filled the coffers while giving pleasure to hundreds of friends on these occasions."[2]

It was impossible for Susa to "forget" whose daughter she was. Brigham's life, values, experiences, and stories of the early Saints in Kirtland, Missouri, and Nauvoo were ingrained in her very bones.

Her spirit was interwoven with those who had gone before, and she often expressed a deep respect, a wonderment, at the majestic courage and dedication of these "first Saints."

B. H. Roberts had made the pioneer journey himself, after the harrowing years of his childhood in the hands of unkind and unprincipled people. He was asked to be the guest speaker on March 24, 1903, at which time he was Assistant Church Historian. He said, "Some of the intelligent spirits in Heaven were chosen to be rulers and to take part in the destiny of nations. So with the pioneers; they were chosen and directed by God to go forth and do this work. Therefore, we should love and revere the pioneers and hold dear their memories."[3]

Experiences like these kept open the spiritual oneness, and both the women and the men of Susa's day were close enough to remember and to feel interwoven with their heritage of what had gone before.

Susa's personal life was full of change and challenges, too. In 1893 she gave birth to a son whom she and Jacob named Franklin Young Gates. Franklin lived to be seventy-eight years old. But Heber, born the following year, did not live the year out, and little Brigham Young Gates, born in 1896, survived only until 1900 and died at the tender age of four. Her children suffered different, almost freakish deaths—one of dye poisoning from a candy wrapper; one, while playing with a friend, was accidentally shot to death.

The year 1893 also marked the horrifying accidental death of her son, Bailey, in a factory explosion. This son, whom she had held close to herself and cherished, only to have been forced to watch him torn away from her when she went with her husband to the Sandwich Islands—this lovely boy, on the verge of manhood, was suddenly snatched away.

Susa must come to grips with these sufferings, else they would mar her life and the progress of her spirit forever. In Volume IV, Number 12, of the *Young Woman's Journal,* September 1893, Susa had written the editorial "Not My Will," sharing the sacred depths of her hard-won commitment, which had come through much anguish, longing, prayer, and faith. There is nothing more tender or powerful in all the writings of the Church. Expanding her theme, she wrote:

> Sickness, thank God for that; health, thank God for that; poverty, thank God for that; wealth and pleasure, thank God for that. . . . If Death raps at my door, thank God for that. If only I, this cumbersome, heavy, willful, disobedient I, can keep the laws of God, what is anything that happens to me? Nothing but a providence of God, and therefore to be received joyfully.[4]

So, what have we in terms of harsh realities? Susa was already heavily involved on several fronts, from the BYU Board of Trustees and the Press Club, to her role in founding Daughters of Utah Pioneers—Young Women General Board, to her breathing into life and canvassing tirelessly that the *Young Woman's Journal* might become a reality. But that reality, perhaps more than anything else, was a month by month draining of her resources, insights, experiences and brilliant organization, which gathered in the cream of LDS men and women to speak their hearts and to give counsel and encouragement to the youth of the Church. During this time she went through three pregnancies, three births, and the death of her pure infant son in 1894, before he had really begun his life. Mixed in was her establishment in 1897 of the BYU Domestic Arts Department—an incredibly innovation breakthrough, especially for the girls of the Church.

Susa's sweet Sarah Beulah was six years old at this time, capable of helping her mother, as well as generally taking care of herself. Before Brigham Young Gates died in 1900, as a vivacious and quick-minded little boy, Susa had also assisted in organizing the Utah Chapter of Daughters of the American Revolution. Also during this time she became a charter member of the National Household Economic Association, and she continued speaking in women's conferences, at times on the topic of "Equal Moral Standards for Men and Women." This was a very brave, and probably unpopular, topic for Susa to speak upon and openly support.

Little Brigham had been born in 1896, two years after the birth and death of Heber. In 1898 Susa's beloved Sarah died at the age of seven, leaving her only one daughter, Emma Lucy, who was both hers and Jacob's, and also her firstborn, Leah, who was opening her arms to her mother again.

She was only human. And, more than that, her creative spirit suffered with a depth of intensity known to few. Her struggles were essential to her continued spiritual well-being and to her ability to give and serve, as she desired to do. Susa knew this. That was why she was able to write what she did to the Young Women; that was why she was able to go on.

At the turn of the century what was perhaps inevitable happened: Susa suffered a complete nervous and physical breakdown. This initially kept her from completing another mission which she and Jacob had been called on in 1902.

With the courage of her convictions, Susa had refused the offer to become secretary of the National Woman's Rights Organization, because the condition was that she say nothing about her religion while holding the post. But she had somehow been selected as the only American delegate to the Copenhagen International Woman's Rights Conference and, while there, she was taken suddenly ill, so ill that she had to stay confined at a friend's house in Geneva for several long weeks, until missionaries gave her a blessing which enabled her to travel to England where some of her family waited.

Did she realize that her condition was so critical? Her son-in-law, John A. Widtsoe, said, "She was ready to die, or at least we thought so." But this was far from the outcome the Lord had in mind: "Francis M. Lyman, an Apostle and president of the European Mission, gave her a blessing. Certain she would die, he began with an admonition not to fear death. Suddenly he stopped, and, as Gates recalled later, waited for nearly two minutes before he continued, 'There has been a council held in heaven, and it has been decided you shall live to perform temple work, and you shall do a greater work than you have ever done before.'"[5]

Susa was already interested in genealogy; even her part in founding the Daughters of Utah Pioneers had helped with that. But the flame had not really been lit, and the pathway not really opened.

We can vividly picture the struggle Susa went through—well enough to travel home, but "horribly emaciated and weighing only eighty-five pounds, she continued to fight for life. When she next went to the temple, she had to be carried in a chair."[6]

But now what a work was to be seen. As she recovered and strengthened she gave her all to genealogy and temple work, adding another tenth of her income in addition to tithing, that it might be used for this genealogical work. For nearly thirty years, until her death in 1933, this would be her great love, the passion of her life.

She was Susa. She was Brigham Young and Lucy Bigelow's daughter. She learned much from what she suffered. With her birthday being March 18, 1856, she was just turning forty-five years old—young enough that her body could still fight the battle which wearied even her indomitable spirit.

As to that spirit, Susa rededicated herself to those demanding principles which she had already proclaimed in the pages of the *Young Woman's Journal*: "Dearest sisters, if we can only put ourselves unreservedly in the hands of our Heavenly Father, we are sure to learn so much more rapidly and happily all the lessons we have come here to learn. And it is such happiness to know, not to think or suppose, but to know that God will order all things for our best good. . . . All and more than I prayed for came, only in the Lord's time, not mine."[7]

Again and again Susa revealed the process that she had been clinging to and the constantly increasing testimony that her efforts brought: "I disciplined my tastes, my desires and my impulses," she wrote, "severely disciplining my appetite, my tongue, my acts—and how I prayed!"[8]

When Susa returned from Copenhagen and then London in 1902, her mother, Lucy, was living in Salt Lake and must have been one whose patient strength and assistance made a difference in those first faltering months. Leah, born in 1874 in St. George, was now a woman nearly thirty years old. Emma Lucy, also born in St. George in 1882, was just reaching twenty, and Cecil, born in 1887, was nearing the end of his teenage years.

In 1885 Susa had written and published *Lydia Knight's History*, a wonderful contribution which just whetted her literary appetite. Not until 1910 would she write a novel entitled *John Steven's Courtship*. But the year before she would begin writing and preparing lesson manuals on genealogy for the Church, and in 1911, when appointed to the

General Board of the Relief Society, she also wrote a lengthy, detailed, brilliant *History of the Young Ladies Mutual Improvement Association.*

She still sat and served on what seemed like endless boards. Two of these expired in the year 1911, but some would go on until 1917, among these the newly appointed member on the Relief Society Board, which calling would last to 1922. In 1905–1908 Susa became president of the Daughters of Utah Pioneers Association, and the timing was just right. She attached conditions to her acceptance: "that the organization inaugurate a program for more effectively training the women in genealogy and encouraging them in temple work. The DUP agreed, and Gates was installed in April 1905. She wasted no time in getting started; her first two activities through the DUP were a weekly newspaper column and the establishment of genealogical classes."[9]

How recovered Susa was at this time, how much physical struggle remained as she took upon herself more and more responsibilities, only she, herself, could know!

In 1904 Jacob and Susa moved from Provo to Salt Lake, and Brother Joseph Christenson, who was secretary to the genealogical society, suggested to Susa that she visit the genealogical library and "hunt out the names of the Young family. Susa replied that she did not even know there was a library in Salt Lake City!"[10]

While Susa discovered the rich genealogical materials in the Church library, she also discovered how little the general membership knew, and how little they were interested in the work and education which alone would make it possible for family organizations and family ordinances to progress.

The task she encountered was herculean. But, once she realized that there were no classes in place to teach and assist, and no printed materials or instructions to teach would-be genealogists, she knew where her own work lay. No one knew how to begin, but she believed she could try!

First was collecting family names and genealogies, then taking the initial programs to stakes and wards throughout the Church. Joseph Fielding Smith was Susa's compatriot in all this work. They urged that genealogical societies be established, and even "started classes at Brigham Young University, and instituted an annual 'Genealogy

Sunday' in the Church. Participation in the International Congress of Genealogy at the San Francisco World's Fair in 1915 was a high point in this welter of activity. Yet the difficulty of making genealogical research a high priority in the lives of Church members who were fully occupied with family, job, and other Church activities limited what even the most tireless leaders could accomplish."[11]

In 1894 President Woodruff made a breakthrough policy announcement in general conference, saying he had received a revelation to end the law of adoption, which drew individuals into the family of Joseph Smith, Heber C. Kimball, or other early leaders. Now Church members were encouraged to perform ordinances for their own family lines. As the prophet now stressed sealings along natural family lines, work to trace information about ancestors increased.

In September of 1906 Susa even held family history classes in the Lion House, trying to stir the fire of this important, very personal work within the Church. She and her dear friend, Elizabeth McCune, toured throughout Canada and Utah, visiting congregations and stirring an interest in genealogy and temple work.

It *was* in many ways an uphill struggle. Discouraged at one point, Susa confided in a letter to a friend, "Not even an angel from heaven could induce some of these club women and these successful business men to set aside a portion of their time for temple work."[12]

In another letter she complained, "I have had to take the part of the genealogical work against all others."[13] It was all she could do to keep it part of the Relief Society curriculum, and some leaders suggested that the lessons were too difficult and should "be simplified and emphasis placed on the spiritual rather than on the educational side of this study."[14] As patiently as she could, Susa bore testimony to them of the fact that the newly published *Surname Book and Racial History* would help the sisters to be able to do just that. "All the desired inspiration in the world will not save our dead," she declared. "We must also have information in order to consummate that noble work."[15]

In 1906 a delightful small break took place, in which Susa was able to travel east and participate in the excitement and celebration of raising the Joseph Smith Memorial at the Smith homestead where the Prophet was born. Always there was the awareness of deep purpose, of joy in the things of the Spirit which she had observed and learned so well as a child, in the examples of both her father and her mother.

NOTES

1. Susa Young Gates Collection, letter: Susa Young Gates to to Leah D. Widtsoe. 01/17/30.

2. *Tales of Triumph: The First seventy-Five Years of DUP*, volume 3 (Salt Lake City: International Society of DUP), 17. Quotes taken from "Organization of Daughters of Utah Pioneers," *Deseret Evening News*, July 24, 1907.

3. Ibid., 17.

4. Susa Young Gates, "Not My Will," *Young Woman's Journal*, volume 4, no. 12, Sept. 1893, 569–572.

5. "Coming of Age, 1907–1920" *BYU Studies Quarterly*, volume 34, Issue 2, article 22, 61.

6. Ibid.

7. Ibid.

8. Essays on Mormonism. https://com.byu.edu/index.php/gates_susa_young_ from Person, 212.

9. BYU Studies Quarterly, 59.

10. Ibid., 61–62.

11. Ibid., 59–60.

12. Lisa Olsen Tait, "Susa Young Gates and the Vision of the Redemption of the Dead," Tait, https://www.churchofjesuschrist.org/study/manual/revelations-in-context/susa-young-gates-and-the-vision-of-the-redemption-of-the-dead?lang=eng.

13. Ibid.

14. Ibid.

15. Ibid.

CHAPTER ELEVEN

———— ❧ ————

OTHER ASPECTS OF LIFE CONTINUED TO EXIST. ONE IN PARTICULAR had special meaning for Susa. In 1903 the modest little academy in Provo desired to change their name from Brigham Young Academy to Brigham Young University. There had been a high school in connection with the academy since 1876, before Brigham's death, but in 1895 it was established as a separate department, and in 1896 the college department was added.

The proposal was a bit presumptuous, for there were only sixty-four college-level students mixed in with high school and junior high classes, and even elementary students as well. A bit unrealistically, the school felt it could offer good competition to the University of Utah for becoming a state school.

President Joseph F. Smith urged the other leaders to relent on this, for he did not want to lose control of vital matters that could not be monitored in a state school, but could be carefully watched and controlled in a church school.

Thus, in September of 1903 the name was changed, with the assent of the Board of Trustees, to Brigham Young University. In this same year construction on the Arts Building was completed and the dedication took place.

Further plans were also in the offing. Susa's daughter, Emma Lucy Gates, "sang a series of concerts to raise money to equip the third floor for home economics, and that floor was named the Lucy B. Young Domestic Department—completed in 1904 and dedicated in 1908."[1] Lucy Bigelow, beloved by her daughter and granddaughter, must have been deeply and quietly gratified (which was her way) at this honor, this continuing remembrance of her name.

By 1909 Susa was turning out as many genealogy materials as possible, including lesson manuals, aided by the magnificent efforts of Elder Joseph Fielding Smith. The *Surname Book and Racial History* was a prodigious effort, cataloguing all the races of the earth, countries, cultures, families; hundreds of pages of in-depth, comprehensive material.

Susa's own inner agenda always existed along with the others, as proven by the fact that she wrote and published her first novel, *John Steven's Courtship*, in 1910. The following year, despite being appointed to the General Board of the Relief Society for a ten-year term, she wrote the really beautiful and sensitive *History of the Young Ladies Mutual Improvement Association.*

In her preface, Susa is practical and sensitive at the same time, a combination she often exhibited in her work. She wrote: "Editing has been done by women busy with housekeeping cares; and the contributors have likewise been hampered in the work by womanly limitations. These facts we hope will temper the voice of criticism."

She goes on to name and praise the women whose work and dedication had brought this organization into flower, as a joy and a beauty, and even an inspiration for their precious youth.

She then continued: "Slowly, and in the face of many hindrances and amidst struggling heartaches, the work has taken form. The field was untrodden; no guides marked the way; and the day had many duties. But inspiration was in the labor; it fostered love; and the author praises God who has been her stay in this labor. May the unselfish loving spirit of God's work come to every reader of this history. Susa Young Gates"[2]

Tempered by all she had suffered and learned, this tender witness was a powerful testimony of the high purposes and desires of the writer's heart.

Susa's whole world was full of awareness, intelligence, and change. In 1914 Susa accepted an appointment as an official delegate to the International Women's Congress in Rome. The following year a mammoth conference was held in the Hague, with the women organizing resolutions and cooperative activities, doing all they could do bring about any semblance of unity or peace as the wings of an international war spread their black shadows over the nations of the earth.

This same year of 1914 Susa organized, edited, and brought into life another new publication called *Relief Society Magazine,* which from the time of its inception became the official monthly publication, replacing the *Woman's Exponent,* which had nobly served a like purpose from 1872 until 1914. Susa served as editor from 1914 to 1922 and was followed in what was in truth a calling by many noble and capable women. The publication was actually owned by the General Board of the Relief Society for its entire fifty-six years of existence and grew from forty-four black and white pages into eighty pages beautifully enhanced with color.

"In the first issue, President Joseph F. Smith expressed his hope that the magazine would be 'entrenched about by the bulwarks of worthy and capable endeavor and enduring truth.'"[3]

This magazine became very beloved by the sisters of the Church throughout its publication lifetime. In 1970, when it was, with some regret to its readers, incorporated into the general magazine for adults called the *Ensign,* the magazine had 301,000 subscribers![4]

Susa's creative juices would not give her peace, and again, in 1915, she wrote a novel with the title of *The Prince of Ur,* which was published first in serial form in the *Relief Society Magazine,* as *John Stevens' Courtship* had been in the *Deseret News* in 1909. Both of these she published under her familiar pen name Homespun.

With Susa nothing was ever entirely personal, set apart from the whole, especially where the gospel and the Saints were concerned. She not only wanted to write herself, but she also wanted to see a literature blossom, as other things had blossomed out here on the desert, due to the foresight and desire and determination of the people. Surely there were those whose spirits were restless with a need to explore, to discover—their very fingertips itching for the expression that words alone could give. She was looking for it everywhere she went, but it was difficult to see.

"Our young people do not write half enough," she stated boldly in the pages of her beloved *Journal*. "It is of small use to con over a subject and simply repeat in your memory what you have read or heard. Not until you have woven the new thought into the woof of your mind by writing or speaking, preferably writing, is it of real use to you."[5]

Again and again Susa wrote of the subject with passion and persuasion. In these words of insight from Richard Cracroft—who studied her life, wrote of her extensively, and felt she was, hands down, the best writer the Church then produced—we gain important insights: "In everything she wrote is evidence of her inclination to point a moral of some kind, to make of her Mormon readers better Mormons. She recognized the existence of evil and the need for it to be present in Mormon literature in either of two ways: either evil should gain a shocking triumph or should itself succumb to the forces of good, so that Mormon readers could be shown an example of how to merit entrance into heaven.

"Susa Young Gates attempted to preserve the ideals she believed essential to the progress of her community. While it was important to her to keep them alive in literature, it was more vital that they should not die where she believed them to be needed most – in the hearts of her own people."[6]

Two years later, in the midst of her daily efforts and responsibilities, Susa enjoyed a delightful and much out-of-the-ordinary respite.

Elizabeth Claridge McCune was the wife of Alfred McCune, well-known for the sumptuous, extraordinary McCune Mansion he built in Salt Lake City. They both had ordinary, even humble, beginnings in their youth, Elizabeth running a switchboard in Mona and living for a time with her family in the infamous settlement in southern Nevada called "the Muddy."

Alfred became so successful in his business interests, being an early entrepreneur in mining and railroad, that the two decided to follow their dreams, and in 1900 they designed and built a half-million-dollar mansion on one of the hills that overlooked the spread out buildings and lights of Salt Lake City at their feet. It was a fairy-tale dream house. In fact, perhaps largely to satisfy curiosity, Susa wrote in great detail all about the rooms, their appointments, and the rich materials used in them: handmade red-roof tiles from Holland, onyx and Nubian marble, oak, walnut, mahogany and cherry woods, as a few. The home boasted a third floor ballroom with balconies and little hidden alcoves and huge elaborate mirrors. This home was *by far* the show house of the city.

Although Brother McCune was getting distracted by his business and an involvement in politics, Elizabeth opened the house whenever she could to stakes, Relief Societies, Mutual groups, and the Genealogical Society. She would always give to the occasion a sense of fun, once dressing herself and her daughters in colorful South American costumes with which to greet their guests.

Now, in July of 1917, Elizabeth held a delightful retreat for her closest friends, four fortunate women, for a week to which no husbands were invited. Each, upon her arrival, was given "a simple gingham gown, which was to be the weeks' badge or uniform. Not even the married children of the hostess were allowed to enter the doors; one came to take a few snap-shots of the party, but was not allowed over the threshold. Each guest went about selecting her own bedroom and bath, and the busy editor guest (assuming this to be Susa) had a special desk fitted up in the Juliet balcony."[7]

Many delightful activities were planned for them, with a dinner at the end of the week to which the husbands were invited. But, behind the merrymaking, there were deeper things going on. Susa and Elizabeth had served on boards together, and Elizabeth became devoted to genealogical work—which, for both herself and for Susa, included many hours spent in the temple. And when Elizabeth, her husband, and four of her children traveled to Europe in 1897, a remarkable thing happened. One of Elizabeth's purposes in going was to do genealogy work, and she asked President Snow for a priesthood blessing, in which he said, "Thy mind shall be as clear as an angel's when explaining the principles of the Gospel."[8] She and her daughters went door to door with the missionaries, attended street meetings, and Elizabeth found herself combatting the ugly untruths which had been widely spread by a Mr. Jarmin and his daughters. He had once been a member of the Church, and asserted that Mormon women were in a state of ignorance and degredation.

Before she knew it, Elizabeth was on the agenda to speak in defense! The word spread that "the lady from Utah" would be speaking, and the hall was filled. Relying on the promise of the prophet to her, she said: "Our husbands are proud of their wives and daughters; they do not consider that they were created solely to wash dishes and tend babies; but they give them every opportunity to attend meetings and lectures and to take up everything which will educate and develop them. Our religion teaches us that the wife stands shoulder to shoulder with the husband."[9]

This was the beginning of many speeches she was to deliver. And the occasion spurred Joseph W. McMurrin of the European Mission presidency to urge the brethren to consider sister missionaries, for many mission presidents throughout the world had already been requesting them. "If a number of bright and intelligent women were called on missions to England, the results would be excellent."[10]

The Young Ladies Improvement Association held a reception for the corresponding group of Young Men in 1898, and while President George Q. Cannon was speaking to them, he said, "'It has been decided to call some of our wise and prudent women into the missionary field.'" Though very few women had accompanied their husbands into the mission field in the past, "never before had the Church officially called and set apart sisters as ambassadors of the Lord Jesus Christ."[11]

Susa's relationship with Joseph F. Smith and his son, Joseph Fielding, continued. In March of 1889 Joseph F. wrote a somewhat discouraged letter to Susa, noting that George Q. Cannon had been released and President Woodruff was able to come out of hiding— and most of these presidential pardons were influenced by President Cleveland, whose sometimes subtle, but noticeable, support of the Mormons made a difference. For instance, he refused to add his signature to the 1887 Edmunds-Tucker Act after both houses of Congress had passed it. In his letter Joseph F. wrote, "President Cleveland was our best friend and did us all the good that party interests would permit. He would have done more, if he dared. He was a brave man to dare as much as he did. God bless Grover Cleveland."[12] Joseph F. had spent too much of his own time in hiding. He was growing older and felt the weariness of life and its realities felt heavier than ever before.

Susa's most sacred experience with President Smith and his family came when she and Jacob stopped by the Smith home on the evening of Friday, November 5, 1918. It was always a pleasure to enter the Beehive House, where the Smiths were now living. It was the first home her father had built, beginning it in 1852 and completing it in 1854. Afterward he constructed the Lion House adjacent to it, where she had been born. She had many warm memories and feelings from those earlier times. And Lorenzo Snow had also lived in the home when he was the prophet.

But this was a simple and ordinary visit, to pick up a box of apples that was waiting for them. She knew President Smith was ill and seeming to grow more and more frail. Susa was well aware of the sufferings he had endured: the sudden death of his oldest, beloved son, Hyrum M., from a ruptured appendix, then a young son-in-law dying in February from an accidental fall—and in September, Hyrum's sweet wife, Ida, gave way to death within days of bringing life to her new infant. It did not seem possible that now there were five precious grandchildren, orphaned and bereft.

When his son Hyrum died, his father had cried out, "My soul is rent, my heart is broken! O God, help me!"[13] We cannot imagine or re-create what it was like for President Smith as a little boy, not yet six years old, to watch his father, Hyrum Smith, and the Prophet, who was his uncle, ride away to be killed by brutal men. And then he lost his mother here in the Valley, when things were just beginning to go well again. Even then he was but a lad of thirteen.

There were others in his family, as well, who had died prematurely, and now the protracted, inhuman horrors of the war had darkened his spirit, the war that was ending at last in at least a semblance of peace. But more devastation followed, in a terrible influenza epidemic that covered all the earth, claiming millions of lives—in the end more than had been lost during the conflict of the Great War itself.

Many people were keeping to their homes, afraid of infection, so that attendance at the October conference was low. But the prophet, though weak and bowed down, presided at four different sessions and confided to his people, "I have been undergoing a siege of very serious illness for the last five months. . . although somewhat weakened in body, my mind is clear with reference to my duty." These were some-what unexpected and powerful words, and the Saints could sense that he was struggling. "I will not, I dare not," he continued, "attempt to enter upon many things that are resting upon my mind this morning, and I shall postpone until some future time, the Lord willing, my at-tempt to tell you some of the things that are in my mind, and that dwell in my heart."[14]

Susa, deeply touched, wrote to her dear and understanding friend, Elizabeth McCune, and maintained that the prophet would have said more. "If he had been strong enough to do so without being overcome with emotion."[15]

With a tenderness that was not of the world of the moment, the prophet opened his spirit to his people and confided, "I have not lived alone these five months. I have dwelt in the spirit of prayer, of suppli-cation, of faith and of determination; and I have had my communica-tion with the Spirit of the Lord continuously." The Conference Report noted the powerful event which followed President Smith's remarks: "At the close of President Smith's remarks the organist struck a chord of 'We Thank Thee, O God, for a Prophet.' The congregation arose in unison, and without announcement, and under strong emotion, sang that sacred song so dear to the Saints."[16]

He longed to personally share the new light and knowledge he had received concerning the manner in which the Savior could have taught the innumerable hosts of dead during the brief time between His crucifixion and resurrection. Much of this organizing and mar-shaling of the Savior's forces was explained and treated in the rev-elation itself, especially verses 11, 27, 30 and 36 (see Doctrine and

Covenants 138). But Joseph F.'s desire to teach these things in person was not afforded him.

Ten days following the conference, Joseph F. dictated the entire vision to Joseph Fielding, and two weeks later, on the last day of October, the grieving, but in some ways exultant, son read the text at a regular council meeting in the temple to the First Presidency and the Twelve.

The apostles, the servants of the Lord, endorsed entirely the revelation which had been given, and began to make plans for publishing that it might be put into the hands of the Saints.

It was the week following this that Susa and Jacob appeared at the Smiths' door. As the two families sat visiting, President Smith asked Susa to come to his room. "I comforted him all I could in his severe illness,"[17] Susa wrote. She must have been remembering, even vaguely, beneath the demands of the moment, the comfort and untiring sympathy he had given her in Hawaii when she faced the horror of her two little boys dying before her eyes. And way back, when they were children, Joseph F. spent much time in the home of Brigham Young, whose care meant more than she could imagine to the fatherless boy. Thus, the interlaced bonds of mortality were sacred to them.

Susa was perhaps more deeply exuberated by this revelation than anyone else, because of her passionate testimony of the importance of the work for the dead. After Jacob and Julina joined them, President Smith handed a paper to Susa to read, and she realized that written thereon was a transcript of his vision. In her journal that night she recorded, "To be permitted to read a revelation before it was made public, to know the heavens are still opened. How blest, O how blest I am to have the privilege!"[18]

She could not refrain from holding forth on the things in the vision which had especially compelled her: "In it he tells of his view of Eternity; the Savior when He visited the spirits in prison—how his servants minister to them; he saw the Prophet and all his associate Brethren laboring in the Prison Houses; Mother Eve and her noble daughters engaged in the same holy cause!" This was the crowning spiritual knowledge which made her heart rejoice—:"Eve and her daughters remembered!"[19]

Two weeks later Joseph F. Smith died. In the *Relief Society Magazine* Susa made sure that many eulogies from many leading women, as well as her own long tribute to President Smith, be printed. The entire text of the "Vision of the Redemption of the Dead" was also printed, but Susa did not share her own personal experience, which was so sacred to her. She did expand a little by writing, "This is unusual—the mention of women's labors on the Other Side. The direct view of [women] associated with the ancient and modern prophets and elders confirms the noble standard of equality between the sexes which has always been a feature of this Church."[20]

Was this "noble standard of equality between the sexes" really recognized and placed in the forefront, or were the expressions more subtle? At least it is certain that at times, when the subject arose, there was a freedom of thought and expression always extended.

Susa's own feelings and views on this subject, as on many others, was laced with passion and an irresistible vivaciousness of manner. She stated unequivocally that if God the Father and the Savior were in the Grove with Joseph, then Heavenly Mother was also there. And no one ever contradicted her nor made her recant. She also maintained that the "great Heavenly Mother was 'the great molder' of Abraham's personality," and that she "has played a significant role in all our lives, looking over us with watchful care and providing special training!"[21]

The hymn "O My Father," written by Eliza R. Snow, was a beloved and firmly established part of LDS theology, with a story of its own. "I had learned to call thee Father, Thru thy Spirit from on high," Eliza wrote. "But until the key of knowledge was restored, I knew not why. In the heav'ns are parents single? No, the thought makes reason stare! Truth is reason, truth eternal Tells me I've a mother there."[22] This hymn became, and remains, at the heart of LDS belief concerning a Heavenly Mother, and of the feelings this precious knowledge engenders.

In "The Vision Beautiful," published in the *Improvement Era* in April of 1920, Susa states powerfully and poetically the deep meaning the Vision, given to the boy Joseph Smith in the Sacred Grove, inherently has for women.

"The world of men looked out with unseeing eyes into past and future glories," Susa began, "when the Vision was vouchsafed to the youthful prophet in the early spring day of 1820. . . . That wonderful appearance in the Grove, at Palmyra, held in its heart, like the half-opened calyx of a rose, all the promises of future development for woman, foreshadowed by that revelation given to Moses concerning the creation when he saw 'man' created in the image of his Maker, 'male and female created he them.' . . . The divine Mother, side by side with the divine Father, the equal sharing of equal rights, privileges and responsibilities, in heaven and on earth, all this was foreshadowed in that startling announcement of the Son: 'They were all wrong! They draw near to me with their lips, but their hearts are far from me!'" In an age-long darkness and apostasy, woman had been shackled because of her very virtue, tender sympathy, and patient desire for peace.

"Can you conceive, then, what the Vision meant to woman? It meant in civil, religious, social and finally, financial matters, the right of choice: it meant woman's free agency, the liberation of her long-chained will and purpose."[23]

It appears in all the varied work she did, Susa never lost sight of its relationship to the whole. And, having followed the counsel of her father, she knew of a surety, with all her eternal soul, that the gospel was true, that it was an eternal plan created for our happiness and growth. She took delight in the plan; she took delight in the work!

NOTES

1. Brigham Young High School History-From 1903-1920 "A High School Within a University" www.byhigh.org/History/History Decades/From 1903-1920.htm/.

2. Susa Young Gates, "History of the Young Ladies' Mutual Improvement Association of The Church of Jesus Christ of Latter-day Saints, from November 1869 to June 1910," 1911, https://archive.org/details/historyofyoungla00gate.

3. *Relief Society Magazine* from *Encyclopedia of Mormonism*; https://com.byu.edu/index.php?title=Relief_Society Magazine / oldict=2775

4. Ibid.

5. Susa Young Gates, *Young Woman's Journal*, volume VI, June 1895, 429. Quoted in Cracroft, "Susa Young Gates: Her Life and Her Work," 63.

6. Ibid., 3.

7. "Elizabeth Claridge McCune," MormonWiki.

8. "I Could Have Gone into Every House," 24 August 2018, https://history.churchofjesuschrist.org/content/i-could-have-gone-into-every-house?lang=eng. See also "Elizabeth Ann Claridge McCune," https://en.wikipedia.org/wiki/Elizabeth_Ann_Claridge_McCune.

9. Gates, "Elizabeth Claridge McCune," *Biographical Sketches*, 343.

10. *Journal History of the Church of Jesus Christ of Latter-day Saints*, 11 March 1898.

11. "Calling the First Women Missionaries," *Church History in the Fulness of Times*, Study manual five: The Church at the Turn of the Century, 2003, 45–64. See also Whitchurch and Perry, *Friends and Enemies in Washington*, 221.

12. Joseph Fielding Smith, *Life of Joseph F. Smith, Sixth President of the Church of Jesus Christ of Latter-day Saints* (Salt Lake City: Deseret News Press, 1938), 474.

13. Conference Report, October 1918.

14. Gates, Letter to Elizabeth C. McCune, November 14, 1918.

15. Conference Report, 1918, 3.

16. Gates, *Susa Young Diary*. Church History Library, Salt Lake City. See also Susa Young Gates, Letter to Elizabeth C. McCune, November 14, 1918.

17. Ibid., Diary, November 5.

18. Ibid. See also Doctrine and Covenants 138:39.

19. "In Memoriam; President Joseph F. Smith," *Relief Society Magazine*, volume 6, No. 1, January 1919, 21.

20. Pulida Paulsen, 2011. Quoted in "Heavenly Mother (Mormonism)," *Wikipedia*.

21. Eliza R. Snow, "O My Father," *Hymns of The Church of Jesus Christ of Latter-day Saints* (1985), 292,

22. *Improvement Era*, volume 23, number 6. April 1920, 542–43.

23. Susa Young Gates, "The Vision Beautiful," Book of Mormon Central, https://archive.bookofmormoncentral.org/content/vision-beautiful.

CHAPTER TWELVE

———— ❦ ————

FAMILY LIES AT THE HEART OF THE GOSPEL PLAN: TO EXALT US AS families, that we might learn and live together through the eternities to come. The families of the earth, waiting and watching, were ready and eager for the organization and the ordinances that would make this union and progression possible for them.

Susa redoubled her efforts and, at her right hand, stood the prophet's gentle and capable son, Joseph Fielding, who had been appointed Assistant Church Historian, continuing his work as secretary of the Utah Genealogical Society, which was the Church's official organization, and being ordained an apostle in 1910. Together and separately they canvased the stakes and wards throughout the communities of the Church, teaching and instructing; organizing and encouraging. "Susa and Elder Smith spoke together at genealogical meetings—she provided practical instruction in methodology, and he laid out the theological foundations of the work. Thanks to their efforts and those of several like-minded associates, thousands of Latter-day Saints received training and encouragement in performing family history and temple work."[1] Susa enjoyed referring to Elder Smith as "'the eloquent spokesman' of genealogy and temple work, and also as 'the Apostle to the spirits in prison.'"[2]

In addition to writing what seemed like countless lessons and workbooks, Susa taught classes whenever she could and traveled to England, as well as to the Eastern United States, and she corresponded tirelessly with genealogists throughout the world, increasing her own level of knowledge and skills, perhaps precipitating the class work she initiated at the International Genealogy Conference in San Francisco in 1915. It was almost inevitable that she became head of the Research Department and Library of the Genealogical Society of Utah in 1923. "She personally cataloged more than 16,000 names of the Young family, and was known and acknowledged internationally, as well as nationally, for her untiring, and oft times brilliant, genealogical work."[3]

Not just for years, but for decades, Susa dedicated herself to ordinance work in the temples. Is that not where she had started, under the patient tutelage of her mother? Was not the House of the Lord worked into the very cells of her being?

Challenges continued in Susa's personal life. She had lost her first two little boys in the early days of Hawaii. Simpson Mark died shortly after his birth in 1885, and the following year Joseph Sterling was born. Joseph died in 1891—and this was the same year little Sarah Beulah was born. Three years later Heber was born and died the same year. Two years later, in 1896, Brigham Young Gates was born. And in 1898 Susa's precious Sarah, just seven years old, died also. Susa's other daughters were older, but Sarah was a delightful child who would have stayed with them longer, and blessed the years when she was the only "daughter at home" Susa had. In 1900 Brigham, who had been born in 1896, was taken by death as well.

Surely the devastation of these heart-rending losses influenced the breakdown of Susa's health and inner forces at the beginning of the century. Her indomitable will, enthusiasm for life, and desire to help and lift—to be of use, as her mother had taught her—were a large part of what carried her through.

By 1905 Susa was entrenched in Daughters of Utah Pioneers and setting up some of her first genealogy programs. By 1906 she was writing for two different newspapers, as well as preparing a preponderance of materials whenever she could, and wherever they were needed. The demands of her life were the demands of the work of the Lord, and everything within her responded.

What of Jacob, his life and activities, and the marriage relationship the two of them shared?

Jacob was born in Salt Lake City on July 30, 1854, to his father—also Jacob—who was forty-three years old and his mother, Emma Forsberry, who was only twenty-four. When he was but a boy of ten his family was called on a "cotton mission," and his life changed dramatically. It was in St. George that he and Susa became friends.

Jacob Sr. had been dedicated to whatever service was asked of him by the Prophet or the Church. In June of 1843 it was a little difficult for him to leave for a mission to the New England States. Things in Nauvoo were extremely unsettled, and he, as well as so many others, was concerned about the safety and welfare of Joseph Smith. In addition, his health was not too strong at the time. He knew Joseph well, and the two of them liked to wrestle together for exercise.

When he met the Prophet just before leaving, Joseph encouraged him, "Go on your mission, and we will wrestle after you come back." But that was not to be. On May 26, 1844, just a month before the Prophet's death, Jacob saw him for what was to be the last time. He was on his horse, just a little distance away, riding to Carthage and what would be his death.[4]

As part of the organization at the October conference in 1844, Jacob was ordained by the Pratt brothers, Parley and Orson, to serve as the senior president of the fourth Quorum of Seventies.

Jacob served many missions in Southern Utah, helping to settle and to serve this area of the state, serving on the county court, elected a member of the House of Representatives, and re-elected three times. The counties of Kane and Washington were blessed by his wisdom and faithfulness. Supporting Zion's Cooperative Mercantile Institution, he became director of the Southern Utah Cooperative Mercantile Association in 1868. In October of 1862 he was ordained as one of the seven presidents of the Seventy, a calling he held until his death.

Young Jacob Gates Sr. was involved in a story which has become somewhat famous in the Church, without most of us knowing details or names.

Jacob was on his way to Great Britain to serve a mission in 1849 and decided to take a little detour to the town of Richmond, where he knew Oliver Cowdery was living. They had been friends in the earlier days of the Church and shared many challenging experiences and trials together.

After some minutes of conversation, Jacob could no longer desist, and asked Oliver outright, "'I want you to tell me the whole truth about your testimony concerning the Book of Mormon—the testimony sent forth to the world over your signature in the front of that book. Was your testimony based on a dream, was it the imagination of your mind, was it an illusion, a myth—tell me truthfully?'"[5]

Oliver said nothing in return but pulled out an original edition Book of Mormon and "read in the most solemn manner the words to which he had subscribed his name, nearly twenty years before. 'Jacob,' he said, 'I am a dying man, and what would it profit me to tell you a lie? I know that this Book of Mormon was translated by the gift and power of God. My eyes saw, my ears heard, and my understanding was touched, and I know that whereof I testified is true.'"

Jacob pressed on and asked concerning the angel who had conferred the priesthood upon him and upon the Prophet Joseph. Oliver answered, "'I felt the hand of the angel on my head as plainly as I could feel yours, and could hear his voice as I now hear yours.'"

"'If all that you tell me is true, why did you leave the Church?'" Jacob asked, and Oliver could only offer this very sad explanation: "'When I left the Church, I felt wicked, I felt like shedding blood, but I have got all over that now.'"[6]

Following this solemn experience, Jacob continued on to fulfill his mission and teach men and women who were seeking for the truth the restored gospel of Jesus Christ.

Jacob Forsberry Gates Jr. served in the Hawaiian Mission from the beginning of 1877 through September of 1879. It was during this period that Susa visited him there, and a tender and tentative courtship began. He was twenty-five years old when he arrived home in October and married Susa Amelia Young on January 5, 1880. At the time of their marriage, Susa was also twenty-five. At the end of October of 1885, he was called to the same mission again, and Susa and the children were allowed to accompany him. At this time he served as superintendent of the Church's sugar plantation, which was located at Laie, Oahu. When he was released from this mission he was thirty-four years old.

This was no ordinary responsibility. Before Jacob's coming, from 1865 to 1873, a sugar factory was built, which was able to employ many of the native Saints. A thousand acres were used for farming, especially sugarcane. There were woodlands and pastures to accommodate "500 head of cattle, 500 sheep, 200 goats, and 25 horses. Meetinghouses, schoolhouses, and a number of private residences were erected."[7]

Upon their return, Jacob and Susa settled their little family in Provo. Susa was certainly very familiar with the area, the university, and the people there. It had been part of her growing up, of her coming of age. For twelve years Provo was their family home, and here Jacob worked as a furniture dealer and also served two terms as a justice of the peace.

Interestingly, Jacob served in the Eastern States Mission from 1902 to 1903, closely coinciding with Susa's breakdown and the time of her struggles to regain her health. He served another mission from 1913 to 1914 to Germany—again a crucial time, just as World War I was beginning to break apart the nations. This is also the time when Susa was at a busy peak, getting the *Relief Society Magazine* off the ground and, probably shortly after his return, writing *The Prince of Ur.*

After their years in Provo, Susa and Jacob moved to Salt Lake. There Susa could be closer to the center of her genealogical efforts and her compatriot in the cause, Joseph Fielding Smith. Jacob built his own house, taking pride in the effort of creating something of that character and permanence with his own hands. It was located at 672 North 100 West. Here he worked as a real estate and insurance agent, but in 1905 had the exciting challenge of editing a new version of the Book of Mormon in the Hawaiian language he had learned to love.

In 1920, when they were both in their sixties, the two of them moved just across the street to 709 North 200 West. This became a family house, with Emma Lucy living there during the 1920s as well, and then Brigham Cecil and his wife, Gwenneth, in 1933.

Deep respect for one another, and gratitude for their shared lives and opportunities, marked the path of this couple. Jacob was keenly aware of his wife's gifts and desired their fulfillment as much as she, urging her even way back in the Hawaiian days, to assert herself, apply for work on the *Exponent* and return to the thick of things. Susa felt no restrictions, save for perhaps his urgings to a high standard of spiritual performance in all she did, a constant shifting of goals and desires from self to the Savior, and the sanctity of the work itself. And these expectations, gently stressed by her husband, were, after all, the same as hers.

Susa always maintained, and happily proclaimed when the subject arose, that Jacob was the master of their home. Even her grandchildren would later state, "Her husband held the priesthood; he was her lord and master. His word was law. She always asked him before she did anything, and he always approved."[8]

No more than that need be said concerning the relationship of these two choice and dedicated people. Susa remembered well the example of her father and her mother. She trusted the truth and beauty of this mortal structure of things; she knew how fortunate she was.

NOTES

1. Susa Young Gates, *Vision of the Redemption of the Dead*, 2.

2. Ibid.

3. Plummer, Louise Plummer, "Susa Young Gates," byu-edu-index.php-Gates-Susa-Young

4. Grandpa Bill's General Authority Page. Jacob Gates Biographical Sketch. *LDS Biographical Encyclopedia.*

5. "Jacob Gates and Oliver Cowdery," Rocky Mountain Sunshine, rockymountainsunshine.com/2018/09/09.

6. Ibid.

7. Brian W. Sokolowsky, "Photographs of Joseph F. Smith and the Laie Plantation, Hawaii, 1899," note 15: Berge "Laie Plantation Sugar Mill," *BYU Studies,* https://byustudies.byu.edu/article/photographs-of-joseph-f-smith-and-the-laie-plantation-hawaii-1899/.

8. "Susa Amelia Young Gates," Relief Society Women, September 3, 2010, https://www.reliefsocietywomen.com/blog/2010/09/03/susa-amelia-young-gates/.

CHAPTER THIRTEEN

Her three oldest children became sources of delight and honor to Susa as they pursued the gifts and God-given directions of their own lives.

Leah, whose association had been withheld from her mother for so long, possessed that same inner determination inherited from her grandfather, Brigham Young, and her grandmother, Lucy Bigelow. She studied at the University of Utah and at Pratt Institute in Brooklyn, and was able to attend a summer session at Cambridge. It was here that she met her future husband, John A. Widtsoe, who graduated from that university with honors in 1894.

Leah, or Eudora, was a fitting mate for him. She obtained a teacher's certificate from the University of Utah and was valedictorian of her class. Then, in 1897, she became head of the Department of Domestic Science at Brigham Young University, earning her bachelor's degree there in 1898. Building on the foundation her mother had established there, she instituted a complete scientific course in home economics.[1] She married John in June of that same year, and this is when they lived in Germany while he pursued a degree at the University of Gottingen.[2]

This is when Lucy was able to stay in Germany with them for a time and be of some assistance, for John had been ordained to the office of Seventy and set apart to do missionary work along with his wife. They had a baby to add to the scope of responsibilities before them. But both Leah and John were made of stern stuff.

His life was hardened by trials from the very beginning. He was six years old, with a new baby brother, when his father died suddenly of a knotted intestine. His mother, Anna, made a modest living as a seamstress. But, determined that her bright boy would follow in the footsteps of his father, who was a gifted schoolmaster, she arranged for one of her husband's schoolfellows to tutor him, thus opening at a young age his brilliant mind.[3]

At the same time, Anna was reading the tracts the LDS shoemaker put into her children's shoes. She asked questions, read, prayed, and left her homeland to travel with a group of Saints to Zion. At seventeen John entered Brigham Young College in Logan. After graduating two years later, he headed for Cambridge, and his future began to open before him.

John was a gifted teacher and a gifted writer, and authored more than thirty books. He achieved innovative things in his various educational positions and earned many honors.

Leah knew his heart and the importance of family to him. Though they had seven children together (some sources say eight) only three of them lived to be adults. Her thoughts must have often gone to her mother, in tenderness and an unwonted sympathy, as she was suffering in so many of the same ways that Susa had.

From the beginning, Leah was interested in preserving the established skills and roles of women, and strengthening the home. She sometimes went so far as to hire young students to assist her in her own work so that she could pursue her professional interests, which included women's health, home management, and child rearing. She wrote many articles and even pamphlets on homemaking. And, like her mother, she contributed to the *Young Woman's Journal, The Relief Society Magazine*, and the *Improvement Era*.

She understood the power of a woman's role and the inherent source of joy and fulfillment it brought. But she still advocated the rights of women "and was one of the founders of the Salt Lake City Federation of Women Voters, serving as president from 1919 to 1921. She also participated in the Salt Lake Council of Women, the National League of Pen Women and the Women's Legislative Council."[4]

Despite the incredible demands on her husband's time and talents, Leah knew she was fortunate to be able to enjoy the blessings of wife and motherhood and the fulfillment of her own gifts as a leader and as a writer.

Thus, when John Widtsoe was called as the fifth commissioner of Church education in 1921 and a member of the Quorum of the Twelve the same year, Leah continued in her support of him and in pursuit of her own contributions to the work.

Susa was still going strong in these years and felt a deep pleasure in being able to collaborate with her daughter in writing a lengthy, detailed, accurate, and loving biography of her father, Brigham Young. Leah also wrote, in conjunction with her husband, *The Word of Wisdom: A Modern Interpretation; How to be Well: A Health Handbook and Cookbook Based on the Newer Knowledge of Nutrition by a Member of the Mormon Church; Brigham Young: The Man of the Hour.* In the Joseph F. Smith Family Living Center at BYU there is a room named for Leah Widtsoe, and Utah State has a graduate scholarship in its family, consumer and human development program named after her.[5]

Leah was the first trained domestic scientist in the Church and in the West. She was also a gracious woman, a kindly friend and, "as a girl, strikingly handsome, brilliant and popular."[6]

She more than did justice to her mother's love, prayers, and faith in her!

Emma Lucy was the first child born to Susa and Jacob, in November of 1882, during the early days they spent in St. George. She was interested in music from early childhood but did not study until she was twelve years old. By fourteen she won a prestigious piano competition in an Eisteddfod in Salt Lake City. This got her parents' attention, and in 1898 she was able to study in Gottingen, Germany—when her sister, Leah Widtsoe, was also there, and when her grandmother, Lucy, was able to go and spend some time with her.

Emma was a gifted singer, and this was recognized early in her life. By 1909 she sang for the Royal Opera of Berlin; in 1911 she performed as prima contralto soprano in the Kassel Royal Opera. The

Great War came to cause terror and havoc throughout Europe and end her promising career very near its start.

Emma returned home and found worthwhile endeavors there, singing with the Chicago Opera Company for a while. Then she and her brother, Brigham Cecil, established the Lucy Gates Grand Opera Company in Salt Lake City, thus offering opportunities to many young performers by staging several operas over the following years.

In 1916 a very happy marriage took place between herself and Albert E. Bowen, who was a widower and had twin sons, whom Emma was happy to raise. She was loved by the people who flocked to see her performances because of her irresistible vitality, her gracious spirit, and the sincere interest she extended to all. She continued to perform in the United States and Canada and established a success-ful recording career with Columbia Records, which was a joy to her mother and to the many who looked for every opportunity they could find to hear her sing!

When Emma Lucy's husband, Albert Bowen, was called as an apos-tle in 1936, her own activities diminished somewhat and she spent a good deal of her time teaching and promoting music in Utah and other parts of the West. She tried to help people see that music is an essential part of what we are, that it awakens and strengthens so much within it that can be felt through music better than any other way.

Emma Lucy was often the recipient of high praise. One critic wrote: "Miss Gates is the equal of the greatest prima donnas this country has produced." She possessed a "lyric charm and sensuous beauty of tone." Her stage presence, theatrical ability, and beauty were praised as well.[7]

Some of the praises bestowed upon Emma Lucy include: "She is the daughter of Jacob F. and Susa Young Gates and inherits from her father wisdom and poise, and from her grandfather, Brigham Young, much of his artistic gifts and creative powers. She is remarkably well balanced" . . . "She is an excellent cook and loves to entertain her friends . . . it is said of her that she is a human dynamo; growth, activ-ity, development, progress—all these are the ruling forces of a busy and conscientious life."[8]

"Her final performance was in 1948 at a testimonial in her honor. She died 30 April 1951 amid much acclaim and honor."[9]

Susa's daughters had married two worthy and somewhat remarkable men, and they had brought strengths and gifts of their own to enhance the unions. Susa was grateful for their happiness and for the contributions they were able to make.

Susa's son Brigham Cecil was born in Hawaii in 1887, part of those first trial-by-fire years that so strongly forged his mother's strengths. The Saints, at the time of Cecil Gates' life, had a rich musical heritage of their own, with many music teachers in the valleys and many professional performers and composers. But as the music scene was transformed and refined during the last years of the 1800s, Brigham Cecil Gates was at the heart of it. He contributed richly through the years, composing symphonies, choir music, individual songs, operas for the company he established with his sister, and LDS hymns that are still in the hymnal today. He was one of the thirteen original members of the General Church Music Committee.

In many of the early Utah history books the brother and sister were acknowledged. In "Utah, a Guide to the State" it is written: "Two grandchildren of President Brigham Young—Emma Lucy and B. Cecil Gates—pioneered the cause of opera in Utah. Between the years 1918 and 1923, they organized, managed, directed and took leading roles in Lucy Gates Grand Opera Company productions."[10] Then a listing of their history and accomplishments follows.

His earliest oratorio, produced in 1916, was called *The Restoration.* At first it did not receive much attention from its Mormon audiences, but later, when it was reviewed and critiqued nationally, its excellence became apparent. A Mr. Walter Kramer from a very respected publication titled *Musical America* wrote the following after Cecil Gates sent the choral/piano score to him. The praise is detailed and warm: "I want to congratulate you on your oratorio, which you have so kindly let me look over. I have been over the work carefully, and I find in it a real sense of oratorio style, admirable musicianship, and inspiration as well. There are parts in it that are worthy of Chopin. It has the best counterpoint and fugal work I have seen in any contemporary composers. Your fugal chorus is splendid and will surely sound well, and the whole plan of the work appeals to me very strongly."[11]

High and well-earned praise; but essential to the music is the libretto, and can anyone understand the deep thrill it was for Susa to be given this opportunity to intermingle her gifts and testimony with those of her son—to be asked to imbue the music with the corresponding life of words? She was actually creating the first "American oratorio to tell a local contemporary history of any kind.[12]

Early Church history was not that far removed from Susa's life. Many of the Saints who had known Joseph in Nauvoo were still alive, living in Salt Lake City or other Utah settlements. Susa, herself, was born a scant twelve years after the martyrdom to a father whose love and loyalty to the Prophet Joseph were a deep, sacred part of his being. And, after all, amongst Brigham's large family there were many who displayed outstanding musical talents; music was in their blood. Cecil had attended the Conservatory of Music in Berlin and graduated with honors. His mind and spirit were prepared for what he desired to do.

Most American works of this nature were concentrated on well-used historical, scriptural themes, the current poets not tapping in to the rich historical materials which were at hand. "In his mother's work, B. Cecil Gates found a poet who framed the Mormon story in an original way that matched the audacity of Mormonism's beginning."[13]

Susa's text for a superb tenor solo of the rejoicings of Joseph read: "I have seen my Maker face to face, That glorious, matchless Holy one, Who bade me listen to His Son And be partaker of His grace. Above my head a light I found Descending swiftly here, And from that beaming cloud a sound Enthralled my list'ning ear. The heavenly Twain above me stood. How could my soul fear Him, When He with grave compassion said, 'This is my Son, hear Him!'"[14]

B. Cecil and his wife, Gweneth, had four daughters, all of which lived into the 2000s, and one son, named Brigham Cecil after his father, who died when he was eighteen years old. Brother Gates served on the general board of the Young Men's Mutual Improvement Association from 1918 to 1929, as assistant director of the Mormon Tabernacle Choir from 1916 to 1929, and in 1926 as chair of the music department at Utah State University and on the musical faculty of the University of Utah. "His settings of hymns such as 'The Lord's Prayer' and 'My Redeemer Lives' have become standards in the libraries of musical organizations throughout the world and are still in demand many years after their first publication."[15]

The family faced a long, grueling crisis when Cecil's health suffered a breakdown in the late 1920s. He had sold the copyrights to many of his songs for next to nothing, but he needed money, for even the Opera Company ended when the Salt Lake Theatre was closed, and all they had poured into that enterprise was now lost. This was on the eve of the Great Depression, and he was no longer able to teach and earn.

His illness posed a mystery for the doctors who tried unsuccessfully to diagnose it. Eventually he was paralyzed and confined to a wheelchair. But his spirits never deserted him. Brother Gates possessed the patient stamina of her forebears. When he needed to compose, he would call one of his children to wheel him up close to the piano. Then he would play the simple melody while the child wrote out the manuscript.

With desperation as well as purpose, Cecil organized a publishing company that could license and protect his music, and this was a turning point in his financial affairs.

Cecil Gates died on August 31, 1941. His brother-in-law, Albert Bowen, said at his funeral: "For a decade or more he lay, although under tender care, helpless physically. The ordinary man under such an affliction would have taken license and said, 'I am defeated. Life's purpose for me is ended.' But B. Cecil, with a grand courage, converted his disability into victory. Some of the finest work that he produced he did while under this serious physical handicap."[16]

Lucy's children added greatly to the richness of her life; they were among the highest blessings God had given her. She always went forward with gratitude like a light to her heart and a lilt to her step.

"Susa was hard to resist. She described herself as '5'3", 115 pounds, with dark blue or grey eyes and light, rather curly brown hair. I must confess my teeth are the only redeeming feature of my face.'"[17]

In a tongue-in-cheek manner, Susa was often referred to, even by one of the Church authorities, as the Thirteenth Apostle, and she was the only woman who had a small office of her own in the Church Office Building. Her gifts and talents are still recognized today. Richard Cracroft, BYU professor, has published extensively about early women writers in the Church and about Susa in particular, calling her "the most versatile and prolific LDS writer ever to take up the pen in defense of her religion!"

It was legitimate; *She* was legitimate, from a realistic, productive standpoint. Susa was trusted as well as respected on every hand. She would accept any work that was given her, no matter how many responsibilities she already carried, no matter how weary her mind and body might be. Her vision was wide and all-encompassing. Her desire was to help, serve, enable, and lift. Her mother, and others after her, had taught Susa well, by example as well as precept, that self-glory must never be part of the incentive where the work of the Lord was concerned.

Love and faith were her by-words, and her spirit was interwoven with them, infusing her legacy. *Faith in the Will of the Lord* had been her banner cry from her earliest days of suffering and illumination— the spiritual illumination she had chosen, of her own free will, to seek, learn, and embrace.

In her mind there was no room for doubt or hesitation, of vacillating toward the entrapment, confusion, and weakness that come from embracing the teachings of the world. In her own words—forthright and to the point:

"What is a mission? Is it not the fulfilling of some pre-ordained plan? Then we know we should have work to do upon earth. And what you're your great charge, your great work on earth? The first duty of a woman upon this earth, the work required at her hands, is that of wife and mother.

"If you cannot fulfill your mission here, He will not withhold that happiness and privilege from you in eternity. Think of it well! The gospel is yours, and by its light is revealed the beautiful hereafter, in which you know you will have the God-given companionship designed for you from before the beginning of this world. Is not this glorious, perfect companion worth waiting for? What work in the meantime is there for these lovely, loving girls? Oh so much. All sorts and kinds of occupation and avocations.

"If you by faith and prayer have succeeded in finding the good and honorable man God meant you to find, then remember those solemn words of warning given by Brigham Young, 'Wife, mother, and then woman.' This is your watchword. And if, dearest and best of Mormon girls, your life is to be lived out alone while on this sphere, choose some good, some worthy object of spiritual and physical activity. If you cannot fulfill that mission with your own body while on earth, yet labor with your whole might to help those who are doing this work.

"Help all good women who know you, and to every child who crosses your path, be thou to it a second mother. No matter what you choose, see to it that you never lose sight of your eternal watchword."[18]

There is the love and yearning of a pure and devoted spirit in these words that cannot be mistaken or misunderstood!

When Susa died on May 27, 1933, she had reached the age of seventy-seven. She was one year older than her father, Brigham, had been when he died in August of 1877. Lucy Bigelow, born in October of the year the Church was organized (1830), died in 1905 at the age of seventy-four. Jacob would live on and die at the end of January 1942 at the age of eighty-seven, living ten years longer than Susa did.

The *Salt Lake Tribune*, on Monday morning, May 29, 1933, printed the following obituary:

UTAHNS TO PAY LAST RESPECTS TO SUSA GATES

Funeral will Be Held Monday Noon in Assembly Hall
Utahns from all walks of life will pay their final tribute to the beloved "Aunt Susa," Mrs. Susa Young Gates, at the funeral services Monday noon from the assembly hall in the temple grounds. Mrs. Gates, second daughter of Brigham Young, will be laid at rest in the Provo City cemetery.

The LDS Church, which Mrs. Gates served faithfully through-out her life, will pay its honor through President Heber J. Grant and Anthony W. Ivins, first counselor in the first presidency.

President Grant, President Ivins, Joseph Christenson and A. E. Bowen, a son-in-law, will speak at the services, which will be presided over by Bishop Gordon Taylor Hyde of the Ensign ward.

The hymn "I've Seen My Maker Face to Face," the words of which were written by Mrs. Gates, will be sung by Richard P. Condie. B. Cecil Gates, a son of Mrs. Gates, is the composer.

The Tabernacle Choir will sing "Come, Let Us Rejoice in the Day of Salvation," "Softly Beams the Sacred Dawning," and "The Lord's Prayer."

Hundreds passed before Mrs. Gates' coffin Sunday at the Deseret Mortuary. Friends may call at the home of Mrs. Emma Lucy Gates Bowen, daughter of Mrs. Gates, 255 First Avenue, from 9 to 11 a.m. Monday.

The family has requested floral arrangements be omitted. Harvey Harris Gates, a son of Mrs. Gates, arrived Sunday evening from Los Angeles.[19]

Interestingly enough, the request concerning flowers came from Susa herself, in an endearing letter to her son-in-law, John Widtsoe, in which she speaks of her burial: "Certainly I object to dollars and dollars' worth of flowers, unless it is summer time and there are some wild flowers that my grandchildren could pick, unless it is too much trouble. *I am kind of a wild flower myself, you know.*"[20]

The poet Henry W. Longfellow wrote: "Lives of great men all re-mind us we can make our lives sublime, and, departing, leave behind us footprints on the sands of time; footprints that perhaps another, sailing o'er life's stormy main, a forlorn and shipwrecked brother, see-ing, may take heart again."[21]

And the gentle New England philosopher Ralph Waldo Emerson said: "One moment in a man's life is a fact so stupendous as to take the luster from all fiction."[22]

In tender acknowledgement of Susa one of her Daughters of the Utah Pioneers compatriots said: "Mrs. Gates is very much opposed to flattery or praise, but the author cannot refrain from saying that she is one of the hardest workers, talented and useful women in the Mormon Church today, and her works will live after her to sound her praises to future generations."[23]

NOTES

1. Album, Daughters of the Utah Pioneers & Their Mothers.
2. Wikipedia, John A. Widtsoe.
3. thechurchofjesuschristoflatterdaysaints.org/study/friend/1990/05/john-a-widtsoe-master-teacher?/lang>eng
4. "Leah D. Widtsoe," Wikipedia,
5. Ibid.
6. Daughters of Utah Pioneers and Their Mothers, https://archive.org/details/albumdaughtersofOObyujake.
7. Carol Cornwall Madsen, "Bowen, Lucy Gates," *Utah History Encyclopedia*, https://www.uen.org/utah_history_encyclopedia/b/BOWEN_EMMA.
8. Daughters of the Utah Pioneers and Their Mothers, ibid.
9. Cornwall and Bowen, ibid.
10. *Utah: A Guide to the State* (New York: Hastings House, 1941), 174.
11. "Brigham Cecil Gates," Mormonwiki.com, https://www.mormonwiki.com/Brigham_Cecil_Gates.
12. Ibid.
13. Ibid.
14. Ibid.
15. Ibid.
16. Funeral Service. Tribute to B. Cecil Gates by Albert Bowen.
17. Cornwall and Madsen, ibid.
18. Jan Tolman, "Wife, Mother, then Woman," *Young Woman's Journal*, 5 November 1893, 91. December 13, 2013.
19. Obituary of Susan Young Gates, *Salt Lake Tribune.*, May 29, 1933, 14.
20. Susa Young Gates Collection, 6. Biographical Note, Historical Note, 19–33.
21. Henry Wadsworth Longfellow, "A Psalm of Life," *One Hundred and One Famous Poems* (Chicago: Reilly & Lee Co, Publishers), 123.
22. Ralph Waldo Emerson, *Selected Essays* (New York: The Greystone Press, 1951).
23. Daughters of Utah Pioneers and Their Mothers, 34.

About the Author

Susan Evans McCloud is a prolific and versatile writer, with more than fifty published books that range from historical fiction to mystery, nonfiction, and children's literature. For many years she wrote her own column for *Deseret News* and created many projects and songs for the Church's Young Women, seminary, genealogy, and other programs. She is poetic yet precise in her writing and research and offers outstanding examples of literature at its best. She is also the author of two of our most beloved hymns, "Lord, I Would Follow Thee" and "As Zion's Youth."

Susan has taught English and creative writing at a private school and has served as teacher and area board member for Daughters of the Utah Pioneers. For thirty-five years Susan served as a docent at Brigham Young's Beehive House in Salt Lake City. She has six children, ten grandchildren, and eight great-grandchildren to date.